Contents

Introduction

Over the last two decades, low fat and low cholesterol diets have been promoted as the way to reduce your cholesterol levels and reduce the risk of heart disease. Despite this, cholesterol levels, obesity, heart disease and diabetes have all increased, and cardiovascular disease (CVD) is the biggest killer in the UK.

This book provides the ground-breaking truth about cholesterol. The truth is, that although cholesterol does play a role in increasing the risk of cardiovascular disease, it is not because of the amount of cholesterol you eat, and is not completely related to the amount of cholesterol circulating in your bloodstream. This book explores the role that oxidized cholesterol appears to play in the development of cardiovascular disease, and the increasing evidence that points to causative factors other than the fats that we eat and the amount of cholesterol in your blood.

If you are one of every three people in the UK over the age of 45 taking statins to lower cholesterol, you need to read this book! The effects of statins and how they really work is discussed, but you can also discover other options such as phytosterol therapy and lifestyle adaptations that will really make a difference to your cholesterol levels and your cholesterol metabolism. You'll not only discover the facts about cholesterol, but also learn how different foods, medications and lifestyle interventions actually affect your cholesterol metabolism. A wealth of practical, simple tips enabling you to adapt your diet and lifestyle will help you to improve and manage your cardiovascular wellbeing. Research suggests that a 10% reduction in LDL cholesterol induced by either medication or diet modification could decrease the risk of cardiovascular disease by as much as 20%, so it's worth making changes.

Cholesterol: The Essential Guide tells you everything you need to know about cholesterol:

- What cholesterol is.
- What your cholesterol levels should be – with and without other CVD risk factors.

'If you are one of every three people in the UK over the age of 45 taking statins to lower cholesterol, you need to read this book!'

- The different types of cholesterol – dietary and hepatic, good (HDL) and bad (LDL).

- Which foods contain cholesterol – and why this isn't as important as you might think.

- How cholesterol circulates in the bloodstream, and why this is important.

- What causes high cholesterol, how you can reduce it – and whether you need to reduce it.

- What foods you really need to cut down on.

- Everything you need to know about cholesterol medication.

- Lifestyle and natural supplement options to help manage cholesterol metabolism.

Find out the real causes of cardiovascular disease and dysfunctional cholesterol metabolism – and discover what you can do to help yourself. This book is an absolute must-read for just about everyone!

'Let food be your medicine, and medicine be your food.'

Hippocrates AD390.

Chapter One

Cholesterol - The Basics

Cholesterol is a type of fat found in animals (including humans!). It is one of the types of blood lipid (fat) that circulates in our bloodstream – the other type is called triglycerides. If you have a high level of lipids in your blood – known as hyperlipidemia – this can increase your risk of having a heart attack or stroke. However, although we tend to think of cholesterol as a harmful substance, we do need it for good health, and a lack of cholesterol can be just as unhealthy as too much.

Where does cholesterol come from?

The cholesterol in our bloodstream comes from two sources:

- Cholesterol we consume when we eat foods such as egg yolks or liver (also called exogenous or dietary cholesterol).
- Cholesterol that our liver makes (also called hepatic, biliary or endogenous cholesterol).

Actually, most cholesterol in the body is made by the liver, and the amount of cholesterol consumed has been shown to have little effect upon blood cholesterol levels in most people. If you eat more foods high in cholesterol, your liver should make less to balance out the total amount of cholesterol within the body, and if you follow a low cholesterol diet, your liver should make enough cholesterol for your bodily needs. In some individuals, however, blood cholesterol levels do rise and fall in relation to the amount of cholesterol eaten.

'Dietary cholesterol has a much weaker effect on blood cholesterol levels than saturated fat intake, and the main focus should always be reduction of saturated fatty acids in the diet.'
British Nutrition Foundation.

The cholesterol in our diet only provides approximately 20% of our body's cholesterol – we make the rest ourselves. Some of the cholesterol made in the liver is excreted in bile, which is squirted into the intestines during digestion (this is called biliary cholesterol), and may be either absorbed back into the bloodstream, or excreted in the faeces. Up to 60% of the cholesterol in our body is biosynthesized in the liver and secreted into the bloodstream.

Cholesterol absorption and excretion in the body

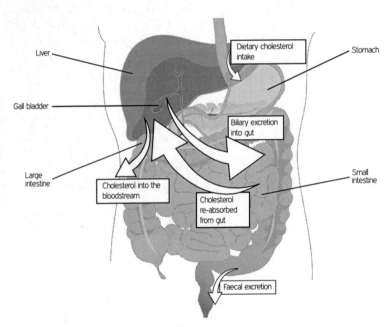

'Cholesterol is found in many foods, but is richest in animal produce such as meat, eggs, dairy produce and shellfish.'

Cholesterol in foods

Cholesterol is found in many foods, but is richest in animal produce such as meat, eggs, dairy produce and shellfish. Fruit, vegetables, beans, nuts and cereals do not contain cholesterol. The table on the following page shows typical cholesterol levels in common foods. Note the highest values for meats, fish roe, prawns and egg yolk, and the differing cholesterol content between full fat and reduced fat dairy produce.

Food	Cholesterol level (mg/100g food)
Meat	
Grilled beef burgers	1355
Lamb kidney	610
Chicken liver	350
Roasted lamb	105
Roast pork	100
Grilled chicken breast, no skin	94
Stewed mince beef	79
Eggs	
Egg yolk, boiled or poached	385
Egg white	0
Dairy products and alternatives	
Skimmed milk	3
Semi-skimmed milk	6
Whole milk	14
Single cream	55
Double cream	137
Cheddar cheese	97
Cottage cheese	16
Vegetarian cheddar cheese	105
Whole milk yoghurt	11
Low-fat plain yoghurt	1
Butter	213
Margarine (vegetable fats)	15
Fish and crustaceans	
Grilled salmon	60
Smoked salmon	35
Baked cod	56
Boiled prawns	280
Cod roe	315

Source of information: McCance and Widdowson's 'The Composition of Foods. 6th ed. 2002'.

How much cholesterol should I be eating?

It is thought that 200-400mg of dietary cholesterol consumed daily is a healthy intake, although in good health, and if you follow a diet low in saturated and processed fats, your liver should naturally manufacture less cholesterol whenever your cholesterol intake increases.

A daily food intake providing approximately 200mg of cholesterol based upon typical portion sizes and average cholesterol content, may look like this:

Bowl of cereal	0
Semi-skimmed milk	6mg
125g pot of full-fat yoghurt	13.75mg
Semi-skimmed milk in 3 mugs of tea or coffee	7.2mg
Jacket potato, salad and small chicken breast	94mg
One 10g portion of butter	21.3mg
Grilled salmon fillet with vegetables	60mg
Total	**202.25mg**

'There's no connection whatsover between cholesterol in food and cholesterol in blood.'

Ancel Keys, Ph.D., Professor emeritus at the University of Minnesota, 1997.

Of course, if you had an egg for breakfast instead of the cereal, your daily cholesterol intake would then be increased by 192.5mg for one egg, or 385mg for two, making your cholesterol intake for the day 388.75mg or 581.25mg respectively! However, you shouldn't need to completely avoid eggs or other high cholesterol foods . . .

1. Consider your weekly intake of high cholesterol foods, and foods high in saturated fat, and don't consume them every day.

2. Remember that in good health your body should be able to adjust to an increased cholesterol intake – certainly if it's just for a couple of days.

3. Consider all other dietary and lifestyle factors that contribute to cardiovascular disease – it's the 'big picture' that counts! It is possible to have a high cholesterol level and yet still have a relatively low risk of cardiovascular disease if other risk factors are not present.

Some experts say that there is no connection between the amount of cholesterol we eat and the amount in our bloodstream, or any association between cholesterol in our diet and cardiovascular disease. More recent research is also suggesting that there are other factors to consider when assessing the cause of heart disease.

Despite some schools of thought that cholesterol levels can never be too low, it does have important functions in the body, and your total cholesterol should be no lower than 3.9mmol/l.

Why we need cholesterol

We need cholesterol to ensure normal healthy functioning of the human body. Cholesterol is used for several essential purposes:

- Cholesterol forms part of the outer membrane of every cell in the human body.

- It is also used to make steroid hormones.

- Cholesterol insulates nerve fibres, facilitating nervous impulses around the body.

- Cholesterol is used to make bile acids which help in fat digestion.

- It is needed to manufacture vitamin D in the skin.

Different 'types' of cholesterol and blood lipids

Although we think of there being several different types of cholesterol, the cholesterol molecule itself is the same – however, there are different types of protein molecule that carry cholesterol and other lipids (fats) around the body.

Cholesterol and other fats are insoluble in water (and therefore in blood), so they are transported in the bloodstream attached to spherical protein molecules called lipoproteins, of which there are different types, and each different type can occur in different sizes. Some lipoproteins are large and less dense; others are smaller but much denser. The lower the density of a lipoprotein, the more fats it contains, so low-density lipoproteins contain more fat (cholesterol), and high-density lipoproteins contain less fat (cholesterol).

There are five types of lipoprotein:

- Chylomicrons – the largest and lowest density molecule which transports fats from the digestive tract to the liver.

- Very low-density lipoproteins (VLDL).

- Intermediate-density lipoproteins (IDL).

- Low-density lipoproteins (LDL).

- High-density lipoproteins (HDL) – the smallest and highest density lipoprotein.

Typical lipoprotein structure carrying cholesterol (C) and triglycerides (T) inside

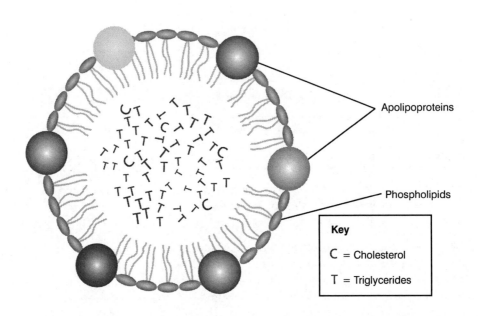

Apolipoproteins

Phospholipids

Key

C = Cholesterol

T = Triglycerides

High-density lipoprotein cholesterol (HDL)

This constitutes 20-30% of our total cholesterol, and is known as 'good' cholesterol, as the HDL protein carrier molecules collect cholesterol from the tissues and bring it back to the liver through the bloodstream, reducing the amount of circulating (and excess) cholesterol. This is also called 'reverse cholesterol transport'.

This excess cholesterol is added to bile and then stored in the gall bladder. This reduces the amount of cholesterol circulating in the bloodstream, and as bile is secreted into the digestive tract during digestion, some of the cholesterol secreted in the bile is carried out of the body in the faeces, hence helping to reduce the amount of cholesterol in the body.

Low-density lipoprotein cholesterol (LDL)

This type of cholesterol is commonly called 'bad' cholesterol because the protein carrier molecules (the lipoproteins) carry cholesterol from the liver to body cells via the bloodstream, hence increasing the amount of cholesterol in the body. LDL is the main carrier of circulating cholesterol in the body – approximately 60-70% of our total cholesterol is LDL cholesterol. Cells require cholesterol for tasks such as making cell walls, and most cells have LDL receptors that take the LDL cholesterol into the cell. Once a cell has sufficient cholesterol it stops making LDL receptors and so the LDL circulates in the blood as less is being taken into the cells. This means that the amount of cholesterol we have in the body is more than we require. Whilst this excess cholesterol circulates in the bloodstream it may become oxidized and contribute to the formation of atheroma (fatty plaques) in the artery walls, contributing to atherosclerosis and heart disease.

'A lipoprotein is a fat (lipid) and protein molecule joined together.'

LDL particles may be large or small, and the smaller, denser LDL particles are more likely to gain entry into the lining of the arteries. Small, dense LDL particles are more atherogenic than larger LDL particles because of enhanced susceptibility to oxidation and reduced antioxidant defense. If these fats oxidize they can cause inflammation and damage, which signals the immune system to try and fix the damage. The resulting clot of immune cells, clotting fibres and oxidized fats creates a plaque within the artery wall. It is thought that very small LDL particles are an independent predictor of myocardial infarction (heart attack). The size, density, degree of glycosylation and oxidation of LDL molecules should also be considered when measuring cardiovascular risk, rather than just the amount of circulating LDL cholesterol.

Very low-density lipoprotein (VLDL)

This type of cholesterol makes up approximately 10-15% of total cholesterol and part of it is converted into LDL cholesterol. Therefore, the more VLDL cholesterol we have circulating in our body, the more LDL we are likely to form, so high levels of this type of cholesterol are considered to be unhealthy. Very low-density cholesterol is secreted from the liver and transports triglycerides (fats) to adipose and muscle tissue. Once the triglyceride is removed from the VLDL molecule, this smaller molecule is known as a VLDL remnant and is either taken up by liver LDL receptors, or becomes a particle of intermediate-density lipoprotein (IDL).

Intermediate-density lipoprotein (IDL)

Some intermediate-density lipoproteins return to the liver but others are converted into low-density lipoproteins, so as these also play a part in the formation of the 'bad' LDL cholesterol, high levels of IDL are also considered less desirable for healthy cholesterol balance.

Simplified cholesterol metabolism

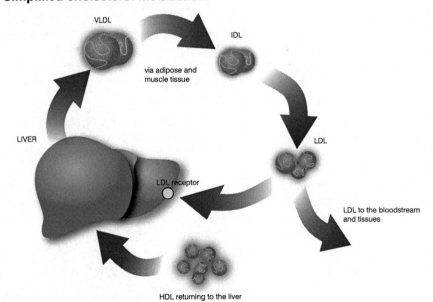

VLDL

IDL

via adipose and
muscle tissue

LIVER

LDL

LDL receptor

LDL to the bloodstream
and tissues

HDL returning to the liver

Total cholesterol

This is the sum of the HDL, LDL, IDL and VLDL cholesterol circulating in your bloodstream. A total cholesterol reading is the figure you are most likely to be given by your doctor, or by self-testing kits, although your GP will have a full breakdown of each type of cholesterol, and some testing kits also show HDL cholesterol levels.

Types of fat in the blood

HDL cholesterol	Good
LDL cholesterol	Bad
IDL cholesterol	Bad
VLDL cholesterol	Bad
Triglycerides	Bad

Apolipoproteins

Apolipoproteins are proteins that bind fats together to form lipoproteins. These apolipoproteins act as 'keys' for cholesterol receptors on cell membranes, enabling the delivery of cholesterol to the body cells. Results from some epidemiological studies and statin trials suggest that levels of certain circulating apolipoproteins may be a better indicator of cardiovascular disease than LDL cholesterol levels, as apolipoprotein (b) (ApoB) levels gives an estimate of the total LDL, IDL and VLDL levels in the body.

Triglycerides

If you have a full blood lipid test, your level of triglycerides will be measured in addition to cholesterol. Triglycerides are the 'building block' of fats, and are found in fatty foods such as full-fat dairy produce, oils and meat. We also produce triglycerides in the body from our own fat stores and in the liver. We

'VLDL, IDL and LDL cholesterol are collectively referred to as 'non-HDL cholesterol' and are thought to increase the risk of cardiovascular disease.'

use triglycerides for energy, but excess triglycerides are stored in the body as adipose tissue (fat), and high blood triglyceride levels increase the risk of cardiovascular heart disease.

You are likely to have a high blood triglyceride level if you:

- Eat a lot of fatty foods.

- Eat a lot of sugary foods.

- Drink a lot of alcohol.

- Are overweight.

Although sugars don't contain fat (or cholesterol), many sugary foods such as cakes, chocolates and biscuits contain products such as butter or cream, and therefore have a high fat content. Also, even though sugar doesn't contain fat, excess sugar can be turned into fat in the body, and increase your triglyceride levels. High triglyceride levels – either in the bloodstream or stored as adipose tissue (body fat) – contribute to many chronic diseases such as obesity, diabetes, osteoporosis and cancer as well as heart disease.

However, although the amount of cholesterol and triglycerides in your blood is still thought to be important, the ratio of good (HDL) cholesterol to bad (LDL) cholesterol is equally important.

Cholesterol testing

Cholesterol is measured through a blood test, either through a finger prick sample such as in a home test kit, or through a blood sample taken by your doctor and sent for laboratory analysis. It is measured in millimoles per litre of blood (mmol/l). The amount of cholesterol circulating in your bloodstream can vary quite a lot throughout the day, from day to day, or in response to various lifestyle activities such as exercise, so more than one reading will provide a more accurate picture of your cholesterol levels. This is especially important if you or your doctor is considering starting cholesterol medication.

Cholesterol testing kits

If you have elevated cholesterol, you are likely to have regular check-ups with your GP to monitor your blood lipids. However, self-test kits are also readily available. Cholesterol testing kits generally contain a sealed test, a lancet to pin prick the finger, a plaster and a set of instructions. Some test kits show total cholesterol, others give both total and HDL cholesterol levels, so you can calculate your cholesterol ratio. Results on most kits show low, okay or high levels.

Does it matter when I measure my cholesterol?

Food or drink consumed within the previous 12 hours can affect the blood cholesterol reading in some individuals, so cholesterol tests may advise you to fast for approximately 12 hours beforehand, or do the test on an empty stomach. Triglyceride levels are more affected than cholesterol by your last meal, so you are more likely to have to fast if you are having a full lipid profile test including both cholesterol and triglyceride measurements. However, after analyzing data from over 300,000 people, researchers at the University of Cambridge concluded that results from non-fasted patients predicted heart and circulatory disease risk as accurately as those from fasted patients.

If your cholesterol levels are high or unusually low, you should consult your GP for further tests.

Should I get my cholesterol checked?

Current UK guidelines advise that the following people should be assessed to find out their cardiovascular health risk, which includes a blood cholesterol check:

▪ All adults aged 40 or over.

▪ Adults of any age who have a strong family history of early cardiovascular disease (heart disease or stroke in male relatives before age 55, or in female relatives before age 65), or a first-degree relative (parent, brother, sister, child) with familial hypercholesterolaemia.

If you have already been diagnosed with cardiovascular disease or diabetes then cardiovascular health risk will have already been assessed and you will have regular blood lipid checks. If you think your cholesterol may be high, you should seek advice from your doctor.

What should your cholesterol levels be?

Recommended cholesterol level guidelines according to The National Institute for Health and Clinical Excellence (NICE) and the Department of Health are:

- Total cholesterol – less than 5.0mmol/l
- LDL cholesterol – less than 3.0mmol/l
- HDL cholesterol – higher than 1.5mmol/l

However, if you are in a higher risk category for coronary heart disease, some experts recommend that you maintain a lower cholesterol level:

'Cholesterol levels naturally rise with age.'

- Total cholesterol – less than 4.0mmol/l
- LDL cholesterol – less than 2.0mmol/l
- HDL cholesterol – higher than 1.0 mmol/l
- Triglyceride level – less than 1.7 mmol/l.

Your risk of death from heart disease doubles if your total cholesterol rises 1.3mmol/l above the upper limit of 5.2mol/l, or if LDL levels rise by 1.3mmol/l from a healthy level, or if HDL reduces by 0.5mmol/l from a healthy level.

The importance of HDL: LDL balance

Your ratio of good to bad cholesterol is considered to be more important than your overall cholesterol level, although total cholesterol is considered to be a reasonably good indicator of overall blood lipid levels and cardiovascular risk. High levels of high-density lipoprotein (HDL) or 'good' cholesterol help to counteract high levels of 'bad' LDL cholesterol, as greater amounts of cholesterol are being carried out of the bloodstream and back to the liver than cholesterol being carried in the opposite direction back into the blood and tissues.

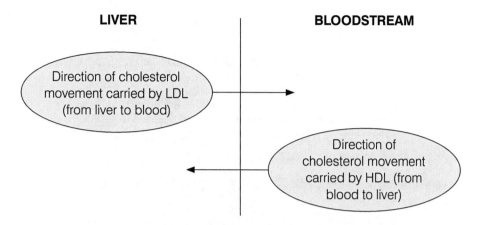

LIVER   **BLOODSTREAM**

Direction of cholesterol movement carried by LDL (from liver to blood)

Direction of cholesterol movement carried by HDL (from blood to liver)

As shown in the diagram above, if your HDL: LDL ratio is favourable (a high HDL level and a low LDL level), then there will be greater overall movement of cholesterol out of the bloodstream and into the liver for disposal. We do need both types of lipoprotein, but it is thought that higher levels of HDL cholesterol will result in a reduced risk of cardiovascular disease.

How to calculate your cholesterol ratio (and risk of heart disease)

You can calculate your cholesterol ratio by dividing your total cholesterol by your HDL cholesterol. For example, if total cholesterol is 6mmol/l and your HDL is 1.5mmol/l:

6 (total cholesterol) divided by 1.5 (HDL) = 4 (Total cholesterol: HDL ratio)

The higher your ratio is, the greater the risk of developing heart disease as a result of elevated cholesterol and triglycerides (blood lipids).
You should aim for a ratio of less than 4.

However, although having a healthy total cholesterol: HDL ratio is important, equally important is the amount of circulating oxidized cholesterol in the bloodstream, as this appears to be the main culprit contributing to arterial damage.

'It's the balance of different types of cholesterol rather than the overall total cholesterol level that is most important.'

Summing Up

- Cholesterol comes from foods mainly of animal/shellfish origin, but our liver makes up to 60% of the cholesterol in our body.

- It is thought that 200-400mg of dietary cholesterol consumed daily is a healthy intake, although most research indicates that the amount of cholesterol we consume has little effect upon our body's cholesterol levels.

- Cholesterol has several essential functions in the human body.

- Different types of lipoprotein molecules carry cholesterol and other fats around the body.

- Non-HDL cholesterol particles (VLDL, IDL and LDL) are thought to contribute to cardiovascular disease, although it is the oxidized LDL cholesterol that is the main contributor to atherosclerosis.

- Triglycerides are also a risk factor for cardiovascular disease.

- It is recommended that your total cholesterol should be less than 5.0mmol/l and LDL cholesterol should be less than 3.0mmol/l. However, a high level of HDL cholesterol offsets high total and LDL cholesterol levels when considering cardiovascular risk.

- You should aim for a total: HDL cholesterol ratio of less than 4.

Chapter Two

Hypercholesterolaemia and its Effects on Health

People with high cholesterol levels have a greater risk of developing cardiovascular disease. The risk is particularly high if the LDL (bad) cholesterol level is high, and your level of HDL (good) cholesterol is low. As the LDL cholesterol is more likely to become oxidized, a higher level of LDL cholesterol in the bloodstream increases the risk of more oxidized cholesterol. The risk of cardiovascular disease is greater if your blood triglyceride level is also elevated. Cardiovascular disease includes conditions of the heart and circulatory system (arteries and veins), such as:

- Atherosclerosis.

- Thrombosis.

- Angina.

- Stroke.

- Heart attack.

- Deep vein thrombosis.

'People with high cholesterol levels have a greater risk of developing cardiovascular disease.'

What causes high cholesterol levels?

There are a number of things that contribute to elevated cholesterol levels. Many of these risk factors are linked to our diet and lifestyle, so the good news is that we can sometimes reduce our cholesterol levels through making positive lifestyle changes. Lifestyle habits that can elevate overall and LDL cholesterol levels or reduce HDL levels are listed below and discussed in more detail in later chapters, as these habits can be changed to improve your cholesterol profile and reduce your risk of cardiovascular disease.

Diet and lifestyle factors that can cause an unhealthy cholesterol profile

- Eating too much saturated fat.
- Eating the wrong types of fat (trans, hydrogenated or oxidized).
- Not eating enough of the right types of fat (polyunsaturated).
- Eating too many sugars or refined carbohydrates with a high glycaemic index.
- Not eating enough fibre.
- High alcohol intake.
- Chronic stress.
- Smoking.
- Lack of exercise.
- Being overweight.

Other risk factors include poor liver or kidney function, an underactive thyroid gland, diabetes, hypertension and a family history of heart disease. Although these conditions increase your risk of having elevated cholesterol, some disease conditions, such as hypertension, can be positively affected by certain lifestyle changes.

Familial hypercholesterolaemia (primary dyslipidaemia)

However, approximately 1 in every 500 people has familial hypercholesterolaemia, a condition which is less likely to respond to lifestyle changes alone. This is a genetic condition where there are fewer LDL receptors (similar to a gate or door) on cells to allow cholesterol to enter the body's cells from the bloodstream. Most of these receptors are in the liver.

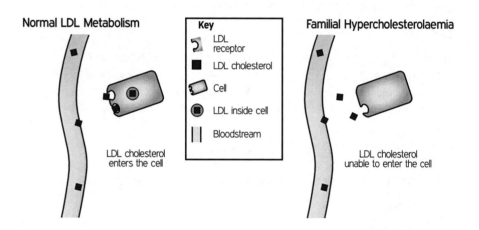

This condition is caused by faults in an LDL lipid receptor gene, resulting in either less LDL cell receptors, or changing their structure so they are faulty, and there are over 300 known gene defects that can lead to this genetic abnormality. Genes (which cause genetic conditions if they are faulty) are proteins that determine how our body is made and how it works. Children and siblings related to someone with familial hypercholesterolaemia have a 50% risk of having this genetic defect which may double the amount of LDL cholesterol in the bloodstream.

This genetic disruption leads to a build-up of cholesterol in the blood as less cholesterol is taken into the cells and remains in the bloodstream. The excess LDL cholesterol in the bloodstream can cause hardening of the arteries (arteriosclerosis) and a build-up of fatty plaques on the inside of artery walls (atherosclerosis) if it becomes oxidized. A gradual build-up of fatty deposits on the inside of arteries begins in all of us during childhood, and deposits generally increase as we age. However, in familial hypercholesterolaemia, this is exaggerated.

How will you know if you have familial hypercholesterolaemia?

Approximately one third of people with familial hypercholesterolaemia experience no symptoms of the condition until sudden cardiac death. However, indications due to impaired LDL clearance may result in cholesterol deposits in or around the eyes, on tendons such as the Achilles tendon, or in the skin.

Diagnosis of familial hypercholesterolaemia

Your doctor will take a blood sample and measure blood lipid levels:

- Total cholesterol.

- LDL cholesterol.

- HDL cholesterol.

- Triglycerides.

Your blood lipid levels will be compared with normal levels for your age and weight, and presence of diabetes, kidney disease or hypothyroidism considered. Cholesterol can increase during pregnancy and decrease within three months of a heart attack, so these factors are also taken into account. If your LDL cholesterol is excessively high, this could indicate familial hypercholesterolaemia, and if both LDL cholesterol and triglyceride levels are high this could suggest familial hyperlipidaemia, although lifestyle and dietary causes should also be considered in both cases.

If your cholesterol is elevated due to your lifestyle, making changes to your diet, exercise and other relevant lifestyle habits, such as smoking or drinking, should help to lower your cholesterol. However, if you have a genetic condition that affects your cholesterol metabolism, these changes are less likely to be effective, and cholesterol medication is likely to be prescribed.

Prognosis with familial hypercholesterolaemia

- Risk of a fatal heart attack before age 40 is significantly higher.
- 50 percent of men and 40 percent of women develop thrombosis (blood clots) in the coronary arteries before age 60.

Dyslipidaemia

Dyslipidaemia refers to an abnormality in blood lipids including cholesterol and triglyceride levels – this could be any combination of the following:

- High total cholesterol.
- High LDL.
- High 'non-HDL' levels (LDL, VLDL and IDL combined).
- Low HDL.
- High levels of triglycerides.

High triglyceride levels and/or low HDL are considered to increase the risk of cardiovascular disease the most.

Primary dyslipidaemia

Primary dyslipidaemia refers to genetic abnormalities such as familial hypercholesterolaemia. How much cholesterol we form and the amount of LDL cholesterol circulating are controlled by several mechanisms, and if any of these control mechanisms fail to work properly, our cholesterol levels are affected. The level of LDL cholesterol in the body is controlled by:

'If your cholesterol is elevated due to your lifestyle, making changes to your diet, exercise and other relevant lifestyle habits, such as smoking or drinking, should help to lower your cholesterol.'

- Hydroxymethylglutaryl coenzyme A (HMG-CoA) reductase, which controls the rate of cholesterol synthesis in the liver.

- Rate of synthesis of new LDL cell receptors.

- Activation of acyl-coenzyme A acyltransferase, which helps to store cholesterol in the cells.

So dyslipidaemia may occur because we make too much LDL, or fail to clear the bloodstream of non-HDL particles (LDL, IDL and VLDL).

Secondary dyslipidaemia

Secondary dyslipidaemia may occur as a result of lifestyle or environmental factors, other medical conditions or medication:

- A diet rich in saturated or refined fats, or too many refined carbohydrates.

- A sedentary lifestyle.

- Hypothyroidism, diabetes, kidney or liver disease.

- Medications such as thiazide diuretics or anabolic steroids.

Whether the cause of accumulated cholesterol in the bloodstream is through lifestyle or disease, excess non-HDL cholesterol increases the risk of cardiovascular disease, and oxidized particles such as oxidized LDL (as a result of increased levels of LDL, VLDL and IDL cholesterol in the bloodstream) seem to increase the occurrence of atherosclerotic plaques.

How does cholesterol increase the risk of cardiovascular disease?

Although many scientific studies show an association between elevated total and/or LDL cholesterol and increased risk of cardiovascular disease, it appears that cholesterol may not be the direct cause. Although there is a small correlation between increased cholesterol and heart disease, it is now increasingly thought that there are other simultaneous correlating factors. One such factor is the amount of free radical damage and inflammation in the body.

Free radicals

Some experts think that LDL cholesterol interacts with free radicals in the bloodstream, and/or within artery walls. Free radicals are unstable molecules or atoms, produced by every cell in the body and also caused by various environmental and dietary practices such as smoking, sunbathing and even exercising. Free radical damage within the artery walls results in reduced flexibility, creating higher blood pressure, increasing the risk of endothelial damage to the arterial wall, and increasing the risk of plaque build-up and atherosclerosis.

Free radicals can be stabilised, or 'disarmed' from being destructive by antioxidants which 'quench' free radicals. Antioxidants such as vitamin E are our main source of protection against free radical damage – it is thought that certain antioxidants can reduce the risk of heart disease.

What increases free radical damage?

- Heated oils which have become unstable.
- Polyunsaturated oils exposed to light/sunlight.
- Trans fats and hydrogenated fats.
- Smoking.
- Exposure to sunlight or UV light (e.g. sun beds).
- Pollution.
- Radiation.
- Carcinogens (substances which alter cellular DNA and cause cancer).

'The more oxidized LDL there is, the greater the number of inflammatory markers.'

Oxidized LDL

LDL in its natural state is usually harmless but it can interact with free radicals and become oxidized. Oxidized LDL is found within arterial adhesions (atherosclerotic plaques), and thought to be one of the main cholesterol-related contributing factors to cardiovascular disease. Oxidized LDL reacts differently to normal LDL with other molecules or cells. It seems to contribute to atherosclerosis in the following ways:

- It increases the adhesion of molecules to the endothelial wall (inside of the artery).

- It increases inflammation and destabilises plaques.

- It increases the growth and migration of monocytes, macrophages and fibroblasts, which are all immune cells found as a result of damage and inflammation.

It is thought that oxidized LDL may initiate inflammatory processes, as there is a link between circulating levels of oxidized LDL and certain inflammatory markers in the bloodstream – the more oxidized LDL there is, the greater the number of inflammatory markers.

Oxidation is likely to increase when you are exposed to environmental toxins such as cigarette smoke, explaining why the risk of heart disease increases when there is more than one risk factor, as shown below.

LDL cholesterol is not a risk factor on its own.

LDL cholesterol + free radicals from oxidized fats or smoking increase the risk of cardiovascular disease.

When LDL is oxidized it can irritate and damage tissues such as the membranes lining the arteries. This triggers an immune response during which white blood cells and proteins rush to the site to deal with the 'foreign body' and heal any lesions. This causes inflammation and begins the formation of plaque, which gradually builds up and reduces blood flow through the artery. This is known as atherosclerosis, and contributes to the development of stroke and coronary heart disease. Hulthe and Fagerberg (2002) illustrated a relationship between the level of circulating oxidized LDL and resultant C-reactive protein and tumour necrosis factor (TNF-α), both elements of immune response in the human body.

Oxidized dietary fats

Fats may become oxidized before they enter the body, through being heated, processed or exposed to prolonged light, and the 'healthy' polyunsaturated fats found in fish, nuts and seeds are more prone to oxidation than saturated fats found in meat and dairy produce. However, different types of fat seem to be metabolized differently in the body.

Staprans et al (2005) found that consumption of oxidized linoleic acid (a polyunsaturated fat) only remained oxidized in chylomicrons immediately post-digestion, and were cleared from the body within 8 hours, with no increases in oxidized cholesterol. However, consumption of oxidized cholesterol increased oxidized VLDL, LDL and HDL and remained in circulation for 72 hours, illustrating that some types of oxidized fat will increase oxidized endogenous (made in the liver) cholesterol.

It therefore appears sensible to limit oxidation (rancidity) of all fats, including cholesterol, as the resulting inflammation and damage to the artery lining (endothelium) will contribute to cardiovascular disease.

> Oxidation occurs when a fat is heated, processed or exposed to sunlight.

Inflammation and oxidized LDL caused by impaired glucose metabolism

A large amount of scientific research has now also linked insulin resistance and elevated blood glucose levels to cardiovascular disease much more strongly than elevated cholesterol levels, with many studies illustrating an apparent causal effect of elevated insulin on heart and vascular disease. In a cohort study of 2,611 patients with arterial disease but no diabetes, Verhagen et al (The SMART study group, 2011) illustrated a higher risk of cardiovascular events as insulin resistance increased. High blood glucose appears to increase the number of LDL cholesterol particles and also enhance oxidation of lipoprotein(a), which may be the link between insulin resistance or metabolic disease and increased incidence of cardiovascular disease. Some experts think that oxidized LDL particles may have greater access into the artery endothelium where they then cause inflammation, with resulting plaque formation.

Remnant lipoproteins such as lipoprotein(a) also exhibit atherogenic actions similar to oxidized LDL and are found in human coronary atherosclerotic lesions. Even HDL cholesterol can become oxidized, and upon doing so, becomes dysfunctional. However, further research is needed in these fields in order to understand any possible links with cardiovascular disease.

Whether the cause of inflammation is through impaired glucose metabolism, oxidized dietary fats or free radical damage on artery walls, the end result is the same – plaque formation leading to atherosclerosis.

Plaque formation

'The metabolic
syndrome is
associated with
a 2-fold increase
in cardiovascular
outcomes.'

Mottillo et al (2010),
Jewish General
Hospital/McGill
University, Montreal,
Quebec, Canada.

Inflammation and damage within an artery endothelium (inner membrane) results in various proteins and immune cells migrating to the area to fix the damage. The resulting scar creates a plaque within the artery wall. This plaque reduces the diameter of the artery (the lumen), increasing blood pressure and heightening the risk of a stroke or angina.

Atherosclerotic lesions develop in three stages:

1 – Dysfunction, inflammation or damage of the artery endothelium (inner wall).

2 – Fatty streak formation.

3 – Immune response leading to plaque formation.

Atherosclerotic plaques within the artery walls are formed mostly from fats and inflammatory cells. As cholesterol is a component of every cell in the human body, it has been suggested that more cholesterol is released from the liver and carried to the damaged area of an artery for new cell formation, creating the elevated cholesterol levels found in conjunction with chronic inflammation (and cardiovascular disease).

Normal artery

Fatty plaque build-up in artery wall

What's the link with cardiovascular disease?

Cardiovascular disease affects the heart and the blood vessels going to and from the heart, and is usually a combination of atherosclerosis ('furring up' of the arteries), arteriosclerosis (hardening of the arteries) and hypertension (high blood pressure).

Atherosclerosis

Atherosclerosis is often described as 'furring up of the arteries'. It forms as a result of plaque formation on the inside of the artery walls. As plaque builds up, it reduces the space for blood to travel through, and this increases blood pressure, which creates even more damage to the artery walls. The damage increases migration of inflammatory cells and clotting proteins to the area, worsening the atherosclerosis and narrowing the artery even more. Although hypertension (high blood pressure) and atherosclerosis are two separate conditions, they each cause the other.

Arteriosclerosis

This is a hardening of the artery walls often found alongside atherosclerosis. As our artery walls are made from the foods that we have eaten, the types of fats we consume and the balance of minerals, such as calcium, affect how flexible our artery walls are. Our artery walls are formed partly from the fats that we eat, but too many saturated or refined (hydrogenated or trans) fats increase the rigidity of the artery wall, whereas polyunsaturated fats from fish and vegetable sources promote flexibility. Consumption of less healthy types of fat and dysfunctional macro-mineral balance (between calcium and magnesium) both contribute to less flexible, rigid artery walls which fail to 'give' when blood pressure increases, making them more likely to be damaged. Smoking also contributes to arteriosclerosis.

'Patients with normal cholesterol levels have the same death rate as those with high cholesterol, suggesting that cholesterol only plays a partial role in heart disease.'

Hypertension

Hypertension is continued high blood pressure. A 'normal' blood pressure reading is 120/80, although this figure tends to increase from our mid-twenties as we age. The higher blood pressure is on the inside of the artery walls, the greater the likelihood of damage and resulting atherosclerosis.

So do high cholesterol levels contribute to cardiovascular disease?

'Patients with normal cholesterol levels have the same death rate as those with high cholesterol, suggesting that cholesterol only plays a partial role in heart disease.'

The only correlation here may be that the more circulating LDL cholesterol there is, the higher the risk of it becoming oxidized and contributing to damage and inflammation of artery walls. It appears that the amount of cholesterol circulating in a healthy body is not the major causative factor of cardiovascular disease; in health, we determine and balance the amount of cholesterol required by the body via hepatic (liver) homeostatic mechanisms – in other words, your liver should control cholesterol metabolism to stay within healthy parameters. However, other factors such as oxidation, free radical damage and inflammation do increase the risk of cardiovascular disease by affecting our cholesterol metabolism.

Summing Up

- Elevated cholesterol levels can be caused by various dietary and lifestyle factors (secondary dyslipidaemia), but may have a genetic origin (primary dyslipidaemia).

- Primary or genetic (familial) hypercholesterolaemia is relatively uncommon.

- Although the level of LDL cholesterol in the bloodstream increases the risk of developing cardiovascular disease, it is oxidized LDL cholesterol that seems to contribute to atherosclerosis.

- Oxidized LDL cholesterol contributes to atherosclerosis by increasing adhesions (damage) on the artery walls and increasing inflammatory processes which contribute to plaque formation.

- Even 'healthy' fats can become oxidized through being heated, processed or exposed to light.

- Excess glucose, other types of oxidized fat and remnant lipoproteins may also contribute to cardiovascular disease.

Chapter Three

How Dietary Fat Affects Cholesterol

What we eat can have a major impact on our blood lipid levels and risk of cardiovascular disease. However, rather than attempt to eat less cholesterol, or even reduce your fat intake, more recent research indicates that a number of dietary adaptations may be more effective at reducing your risk of developing cardiovascular disease, or having a cardiovascular event such as a stroke or heart attack. It seems that the key may not be to simply eat less cholesterol or less fat, but make dietary changes with the following effects:

- Positively affect your cholesterol ratio by decreasing LDL cholesterol and increasing HDL cholesterol.

- Reduce the amount of free radicals and oxidized fats entering the body.

- Increase antioxidant intake to reduce free radical damage and cholesterol oxidation.

- Improve glucose metabolism in order to decrease inflammation and LDL oxidation, so reducing damage to artery walls.

As research shows conflicting opinion as to whether our cholesterol intake, fat intake and cholesterol levels actually cause heart disease, it is important to also consider the positive impact that various dietary changes will have upon other cardiovascular risk factors such as:

- Reducing overall weight and central obesity.

- Reducing the risk of Type 2 diabetes, metabolic syndrome and insulin resistance.

- Reducing oxidative stress in the body.

'What we eat can have a major impact on our blood lipid levels and risk of cardiovascular disease.'

All of these factors increase the risk of cholesterol becoming oxidized and contributing to atherosclerotic plaques in the artery walls, heightening the risk of cardiovascular disease. So, if changing your diet can reduce these risk factors, you can reduce your risk of cardiovascular disease, regardless of the effect upon your cholesterol levels.

What does the scientific evidence on fat intake and cholesterol levels show?

The USDA Continuing Survey of Food Intakes by Individuals (1994-1996 and 1998) predicted that an increase of 100mg of dietary cholesterol a day would increase total cholesterol concentration by 0.05 to 0.1mmol/l, 80% of that increase being LDL cholesterol and 20% being HDL cholesterol. However, reducing the amount of dietary cholesterol we eat seems to have little effect on our cholesterol levels, and studies show conflicting results on changes in cholesterol levels following adaptation of fat intake, suggesting biological and genetic differences in the efficiency of cholesterol digestion and metabolism.

The effect of replacing carbohydrates with different types of fat

A meta-analysis of trials (Mensink and Katan, 1992) measuring the effect on cholesterol and lipoprotein levels when different types of fats were consumed in place of a set amount of carbohydrates illustrated the following results:

- Consumption of all types of fat (saturated, monounsaturated and polyunsaturated) increases HDL cholesterol when replacing carbohydrates, and this effect is enhanced for saturated fats.
- Saturated fat intake elevated total and LDL cholesterol levels, and polyunsaturated and monounsaturated fats reduced LDL levels.
- Replacing carbohydrates with any type of fat decreased triglyceride levels.

The LDL: HDL ratio was most improved by replacing carbohydrates with the same caloric intake of polyunsaturated fats – in other words, this type of fat had the best overall effect as it both reduced LDL cholesterol and elevated HDL cholesterol.

The effects of consuming saturated fat upon cholesterol levels

However, a recent meta-analysis involving 21 studies and 347,747 subjects, to determine the association of dietary saturated fat with risk of coronary heart disease, stroke, and cardiovascular disease showed no association between saturated fat intake and increased risk of heart disease, stroke or cardiovascular disease (Siri-Tarino et al, 2010). As Mensink and Katan illustrated that consuming more saturated fat may increase LDL levels, but also increases HDL levels, the fats that we eat may have an effect upon the blood cholesterol levels in some individuals, but this doesn't necessarily mean that these fats then contribute to cardiovascular disease.

It may be that what happens to these fats next in the body determines whether your risk of heart disease is increased or not – whether the fats are, or become, oxidized, for example.

Adapting the type of fats you eat can make a difference to cholesterol

It appears that changing the type of fat in your diet may be more effective than simply reducing saturated fat intake, and this is more effective when combined with an overall reduction in fat intake. Some research does suggest that eating polyunsaturated and monounsaturated fats can help to reduce overall cholesterol and LDL cholesterol, increase HDL cholesterol levels, and also improve your total: HDL ratio. Palomäki et al (2010) illustrated that, compared to butter, cold pressed unsaturated oil (mostly monounsaturated) in the diet reduced total cholesterol by 8%, LDL cholesterol by 11% and oxidized LDL cholesterol by 16%.

'It appears that changing the type of fat in your diet may be more effective than simply reducing saturated fat intake, and this is more effective when combined with an overall reduction in fat intake.'

Limited effects upon cholesterol levels but reduced cardiovascular events

Research shows conflicting results for the effects upon cholesterol levels (total and LDL) when saturated fat intake is either increased or decreased. However, a review of the effects of fat intake on cholesterol levels and development of cardiovascular disease by Hooper et al (2011) did illustrate as much as a 14% reduction in cardiovascular events by reducing saturated fat intake. As neither total or LDL cholesterol were reduced, or HDL levels increased by eating less saturated fat, this result may be down to other effects such as reduced central obesity and fewer inflammatory markers, rather than any direct effect upon circulating cholesterol levels.

'Research is still providing conflicting results linking fat intake to cholesterol levels, but changing the type of fat you eat does seem to reduce heart disease via some mechanism.'

Key results relating to changes in blood lipids and reduced risk of cardiovascular events, Hooper et al, 2011.

Research intervention	Results
Reduced overall fat intake	Lower body weight Lower LDL cholesterol reduced by 0.1mmol/l Total cholesterol reduced by 0.1mmol/l No significant change in HDL or triglycerides
Reducing saturated fat intake	May reduce cardiovascular events by up to 14%
Modifying fat intake (reducing saturated fats and increasing the proportion of unsaturated fats)	Total cholesterol reduced by 7% Triglycerides reduced by 0.11mmol/l No clear effects on LDL or HDL
Reducing *and* modifying fat intake	Marginal statistical significance of cardiovascular events reducing by 23% Total cholesterol reduced by 0.26mmol/l LDL cholesterol reduced by 0.21mmol/l Triglycerides reduced by 0.27mmol/l

Although there were few significant changes in cholesterol or triglycerides from changing fat intake, there were significant reductions in cardiovascular events such as a stroke or heart attack. The most significant results were shown in trials where overall fat intake was reduced, and the types of fat eaten were modified as follows:

- Reduced overall fat intake.

- Less saturated, trans and hydrogenated fat consumed.

- More polyunsaturated fats consumed.

Whether the small decreases in total and LDL cholesterol and triglycerides was the reason for reduced cardiovascular events, or whether the reduction and/or modified fat intake reduced cardiovascular disease via another mechanism, such as lower intra-abdominal obesity and reduced inflammatory response, it is worth making these changes to your diet. Research is still providing conflicting results linking fat intake to cholesterol levels, but changing the type of fat you eat does seem to reduce heart disease via some mechanism. You could say that it doesn't matter how it does it, but if it reduces heart disease, do it!

Moderating your fat intake based upon the evidence

Although much of the research on the effects of fat intake on both cholesterol levels and cardiovascular disease shows conflicting results, these adaptations will help you to reduce your risk of cardiovascular disease through one or more mechanisms.

Saturated fat

Whether saturated fat increases total and LDL cholesterol or not, eating too much will contribute to obesity and Type 2 diabetes, which are both additional risk factors for cardiovascular disease. Saturated fat is not a preferred type of fat for use in the formation of the artery endothelium; if used for this task it increases the rigidity of the artery walls, increasing the risk of arteriosclerosis, hypertension and atherosclerosis. Therefore, with all things considered, it is still recommended that you limit your consumption of saturated fat.

Check food labels to reduce saturated fat intake
High saturated fat content = more than 5g of saturated fat per 100g
Low saturated fat content = less than 1.5g of saturated fat per 100g

Foods rich in saturated fat:

- Most meats.
- Offal, such as liver or kidney.
- Egg yolks.
- Full-fat dairy produce – butter, cheese, cream and yoghurt.
- Confectionary containing fats, such as cakes, biscuits, ice cream and chocolate.
- Coconuts.

Unsaturated fats

Eating polyunsaturated and monounsaturated fats may help to reduce overall cholesterol and LDL cholesterol, increase HDL cholesterol levels, and improve your total/LDL: HDL ratio. However, this may not have a direct effect upon cardiovascular disease because of the effect upon LDL or HDL cholesterol, but may enhance the flexibility of artery endothelium, reducing the risk of arteriosclerosis, hypertension and atherosclerosis. Eating more fish and nuts (rich in polyunsaturated fats) and foods containing monounsaturated fats, such as olive oil or avocado, has been linked with reduced cardiovascular risk.

However, these fats are at greater risk of oxidation prior to consumption, so take care to avoid processed unsaturated fats (trans and hydrogenated), heating polyunsaturated oils, and limit their exposure to natural or artificial light.

Foods rich in polyunsaturated fat:

- Fish.
- Nuts.
- Seeds.
- Vegetable oils.

Foods rich in monounsaturated fat:

- Avocados.
- Nuts.
- Seeds.
- Olives.
- Olive oil.

Total fat intake

In some trials, better results were seen when the type of fat rather than the overall amount was adjusted. However, all types of fat contain 9 calories per gram and will contribute to weight gain, so to reduce the risk of obesity and Type 2 diabetes – which both independently increase the risk of heart disease – limit overall fat intake to no more than 10% of your daily caloric intake.

Avoid high fat foods by checking the fat content on nutrition labels.

- High fat foods contain more than 20g of total fat per 100g
- Low fat foods contain less than 3g of total fat per 100g

If your individual genetic metabolism does respond by increasing your total or LDL cholesterol in response to fat intake, then it is worth reducing your overall fat intake. Elevated cholesterol in itself may not present a problem, but it does increase the amount of LDL cholesterol available to become oxidized – which is a problem.

'If your individual genetic metabolism does respond by increasing your total or LDL cholesterol in response to fat intake, then it is worth reducing your overall fat intake.'

In order to understand why different types of fats are more or less likely to become oxidized, let's take a look at their molecular structure.

The structure of fats and how they contribute to heart disease

Saturated fat

This type of fat is found mostly in foods of animal origin and is solid at room temperature. It can be used for energy production in the body, but if not used it is stored as adipose tissue (body fat). If it is eaten in excess and used to form cell membranes – a job usually reserved for the unsaturated fats – then the properties of cell membranes are affected. This can affect parts of the body such as the inside of artery walls, reducing their flexibility and making arteries more susceptible to damage and cardiovascular disease. Saturated and trans fats (found in many bakery and processed foods) have been linked with both increased low-density and total cholesterol levels and a higher occurrence of heart disease.

Chemical structure of a saturated fat

Polyunsaturated fat

Polyunsaturated fats are usually liquid (oils) at room temperature. It is this group of fats which contains the essential fatty acids needed for good health (linolenic and linoleic), and the long chain fish oils known to be beneficial to cardiovascular health. This type of fat is naturally used to form cell walls, creating more flexible artery walls. This enhanced flexibility can help to reduce the pressure on the artery walls, thus decreasing blood pressure and damage to artery walls, and reducing the risk of cardiovascular disease.

Chemical structure of a polyunsaturated fat

```
      H   H   H   H   H   H   H   H   H   H   H   H
      |   |   |   |   |   |   |   |   |   |   |   |           O
                                                             //
 H -- C - C - C = C - C - C = C - C - C = C - C - C -- C
      |   |       |       |           |       |   |         \
      H   H       H       H           H       H   H           OH
```

Oxidation of unsaturated fats

Polyunsaturated vegetables oils such as sunflower or safflower oil are not as healthy when heated or processed, as oxygen can easily combine with them, attaching to the gaps underneath the double bonds shown in the diagram. These oxygen molecules are only loosely connected to the rest of the fat, and are likely to separate from the fat once in the body, becoming something called a free radical. As the oxygen molecule attaches to other molecules or cells, this causes free radical damage in the body, so it is best to consume these oils directly from their natural source (nuts and seeds) or use the oils cold as a salad dressing.

Monounsaturated fat

Monounsaturated fat is found mostly in plant foods and oils, and is one of the healthiest types of fat to consume as it contains only one double bond in each fatty acid chain. Only having one 'gap' limits the risk of oxidation (when oxygen attaches to the chain), or hydrogenation (when hydrogen attaches, making the fat saturated), in comparison to polyunsaturated fatty acids which often have many 'gaps'. Olive oil has been shown to have beneficial cardiovascular properties, especially as part of a healthy, Mediterranean-type diet also high in fruit, vegetables and fish.

Chemical structure of a monounsaturated fat

Hydrogenated fats

Just as oxygen can attach at the double bond 'gap' in an unsaturated fat, so can other atoms such as hydrogen. Hydrogenated fats are polyunsaturated fats that have undergone a process allowing additional hydrogen to attach to the carbon atoms with double bonds, creating a man-made saturated fat. This is how margarines made with polyunsaturated vegetable oils can be solid rather than liquid at room temperature – they've been turned into saturated fats. Although use of hydrogenated fats is now being scrutinised due to an increasing amount of evidence that these fats are detrimental to health, many are still used in processed foods.

Trans fats

Trans fats are polyunsaturated fats that have been partially hydrogenated, making the fat more stable and less likely to spoil. This type of fat is often used in processed foods to improve food palatability and create certain food textures, form spreadable products and increase shelf-life.

Trans fats raise LDL cholesterol and lower HDL levels, and are often found within atherosclerotic plaques. They also increase levels of inflammatory markers in the body, and have been linked with increased risk of heart disease, stroke, insulin resistance and diabetes. In a large scale analysis of dietary intake of 85,095 women in The Nurses Health Study (1993), Willet et al found that foods containing trans fats, such as margarine, biscuits, cake and white bread, were each significantly associated with higher risks of cardiovascular disease, supporting the hypothesis that consumption of partially hydrogenated vegetable oils may contribute to occurrence of heart disease.

Small amounts of trans fats occur naturally in meat (predominantly beef) and dairy foods, but they can be produced during partial hydrogenation in food processing, and these types of trans fats have been linked with increased risk of coronary heart disease. The shape of a trans fat molecule is a different shape from a normal fat molecule, which alters the characteristics of the fat and the way that it reacts and is used in the body. Mensick et al (2003) conducted a meta-analysis of trials measuring the effects of different dietary regimes on cholesterol levels and risk of cardiovascular disease, and concluded that reducing the intake of trans fatty acids reduces the risk of cardiovascular disease.

Trans fats that are taken up into the tissues can also contribute to ill health in a number of other ways:

- Hydrogenation destroys the beneficial essential fatty acids, replacing them with toxic fatty substances.

- They interfere with the essential roles of healthy fatty acids, and can affect immune function, insulin control and reduce the effectiveness of liver enzymes responsible for detoxification.

- There is also a close correlation between the amount of trans fats consumed and cancer occurrence.

Types of food containing hydrogenated and partially hydrogenated trans fats

Foods most likely to contain trans fats include: margarines (particularly hard margarines), sauces, gravy mixes, salad dressings, crisps and similar savoury snacks, refined bakery goods (cookies, muffins, cakes, biscuits and pastries), chocolate and fast food.

Proportions of fats in foods

'A 2% absolute increase in energy intake from trans fat has been associated with a 23% increase in cardiovascular risk.'

Remig et al, Department of Human Nutrition, Kansas State University, USA.

All foods contain a mixture of nutrients and fats are no exception. Although we classify fatty foods depending upon which type of fat they contain the most of (for example, we say that butter is saturated fat), fats mostly contain a mixture of saturated, monounsaturated and polyunsaturated fats, as shown below. You can see that the higher the level of saturated fats, the more solid that fat is at room temperature; the greater the amount of unsaturated fats, the more liquid the fat is. This also represents the solidity and rigidity of structures that these fats are used to form in the body, such as artery walls. The higher the amount of saturated fat used in such a structure, the less flexible it is, which can contribute to damage on the artery wall through lack of flexibility when blood pressure rises.

Types of fatty acid in various foods

Types of fat (g/100g)	Saturated	Monounsaturated	Polyunsaturated
Butter	52.1	20.9	2.8
Olive oil	14.3	73	8.2
Sunflower oil	12	20.5	63.3
Margarine, hard	40	21	21.3
Rapeseed oil	6.6	59.3	29.3

Source of information: McCance and Widdowson's 'The Composition of Foods. 6th ed. 2002'.

Need2Know

How to adjust your dietary fat intake for better cardiovascular health

Eating more foods containing a higher proportion of monounsaturated and polyunsaturated fats provides the body with the types of fatty acid needed to create a healthier arterial wall with a higher level of flexibility. Avoiding processed fats and limiting oxidation of fats will help to reduce potential damage and inflammation which could contribute to arterial disease. Some studies do show links between the levels of LDL and HDL cholesterol and the types of fats eaten; if this simply reduces the amount of LDL that may become oxidized, this also contributes to improved cardiovascular health.

Eat more fish

Higher fish consumption is part of a Mediterranean-style diet, and has been linked with lower levels of both cholesterol and triglycerides (fats in the blood). Fresh or frozen fish is the best option, and there are more essential fatty acids known to promote heart health in oily fish rather than non-oily fish.

Ways to eat more fish:

* Swap egg and bacon for kippers at breakfast.

* Enjoy kedgeree or sardines on toast for brunch or lunch.

* Add mackerel, salmon or tuna to sandwiches instead of cheese, egg or meat.

* Have fish with vegetables instead of meat for your evening meal.

White fish such as cod or haddock do contain heart-healthy long chain fatty acids, but these fish store less fat in their flesh than oily fish such as salmon, so there is a lower amount of fat in white fish. The fats in oily fish such as tuna are often lost during the canning process, so tinned fish often contains lower levels of fatty acids in comparison to eating it fresh or frozen. The amount of fatty acids in tinned oily fish is similar to the levels found in non-oily fish.

'The UK Food Standards Agency (FSA) recommends that we eat at least two portions of fish a week, of which one portion should be oily fish.'

Oily fish

- Salmon
- Mackerel
- Trout
- Herring
- Sardines
- Pilchards
- Tuna
- Swordfish
- Kipper
- Anchovies

White/non-oily fish

- Cod
- Haddock
- Coley
- Plaice
- Lemon sole
- Whiting
- Halibut
- Skate
- Rock salmon
- Dover sole

If you don't like fish but would like to benefit from heart-healthy fish oils, take 500mg-1g of fish or krill oil supplements daily. Krill is a type of crustacean.

Other ways to eat healthier fats

Swapping meat for fish is just one way to decrease your intake of saturated fats and eat more polyunsaturated fats. Decreasing full-fat dairy produce and limiting egg consumption is another way to decrease saturated fat intake.

- Enjoy peppered mackerel or walnut-Waldorf salad rather than egg or cheese salad.

- Eat guacomole (made with avocado) rather than coleslaw or creamy dips.

- Spread bread or crackers with guacamole, hummus or tahini instead of butter or mayonnaise.

- Sprinkle seeds or pine nuts onto stir fries instead of grated cheese.

- Add avocado to salads rather than cheese, egg or meat.

- Snack on olives, nuts or seeds rather than crisps, biscuits, cakes or chocolate.

- Cook with olive oil rather than butter, lard, or polyunsaturated oils – fats rich in monounsaturated fatty acids such as olive oil are also less prone to oxidation than polyunsaturated fats.

- Use polyunsaturated vegetable oils such as linseed or rapeseed oil as a salad dressing instead of mayonnaise or sauces containing butter or cheese.

'Dip your bread in olive oil rather than spreading butter or margarine on it.'

Olive oil – cardio-protective properties

The Mediterranean-style diet has been repeatedly linked with a decreased risk of cardiovascular disease due to reduced cholesterol and blood pressure measurements, improved glucose metabolism, and reduced damage and inflammation in artery walls. Although it is likely that this is due to several combined dietary factors, one plus point is the consumption of monounsaturated fats such as olive oil rather than saturated fats.

Summing Up

- The amount of cholesterol consumed has little effect upon blood cholesterol levels in most individuals.

- Research shows conflicting evidence regarding the effects of consuming differing amounts and different types of fat on cholesterol levels.

- It appears to be beneficial to cardiovascular health to reduce overall fat intake and saturated fat intake, although this is not necessarily because of any detrimental effects upon cholesterol levels, and is dependant upon the rest of the diet.

- Increasing consumption of polyunsaturated and monounsaturated fats appears to offer cardiovascular benefits, although this may also not be due to effects upon cholesterol levels, and is dependant upon the rest of the diet.

- Replacing a limited amount of carbohydrate in the diet with fat appears to have a beneficial effect upon cholesterol levels.

- You should avoid hydrogenated and trans fats.

- Try to limit the oxidation of fats by avoiding heating polyunsaturated fats, or exposing fats to light.

- Eat more fish, nuts, seeds, olives, avocado and vegetable oils.

- Reduce saturated fats found in full-fat dairy produce, meats and eggs.

Chapter Four

A Diet to Lower Cholesterol

The biggest influence upon cholesterol metabolism is the type and mix of fats and carbohydrates that you eat – not the amount of cholesterol you consume. So in addition to altering your fat consumption, there are a number of other dietary changes you can make to naturally lower cholesterol levels and have a positive impact upon your risk of cardiovascular disease.

- Eat a high-fibre diet.

- Choose inulin-rich foods (artichokes, garlic, chicory or asparagus).

- Eat foods high in antioxidants to reduce oxidative damage and oxidized cholesterol.

- Eat foods naturally rich in phytosterols.

- Eat fewer refined carbohydrates and more carbohydrates with a low glycaemic index.

Eating more fibre

Eating more high-fibre foods has been shown to help reduce cholesterol levels. This is due to a number of mechanisms:

- Some types of fibre bind with cholesterol in the gut and move it on to the large intestine where it is expelled via the faeces.

- Types of fibre which remain undigested and travel on to the large intestine create favourable by-products during fermentation, and these by-products re-enter the bloodstream and lower blood lipid levels.

'The biggest influence upon cholesterol metabolism is the type and mix of fats and carbohydrates that you eat – not the amount of cholesterol you consume.'

- Many high fibre foods such as wholegrains, legumes and nuts contain compounds called phytosterols, which compete with cholesterol for absorption into the body.

Additional benefits of a high-fibre diet

In addition to directly reducing the amount of cholesterol that you absorb into the bloodstream, a high fibre intake offers additional benefits:

- Fibre helps to regulate glucose absorption and blood sugar control, reducing oxidative stress known to be detrimental to cholesterol metabolism.

- Fibre intake increases satiety (the feeling of fullness) and helps in weight control. There is a link between central obesity and increased levels of oxidized cholesterol.

As obesity and diabetes seem to increase the amount of oxidized cholesterol and heighten the risk of heart disease, dietary changes that help to reduce the risk of these diseases as well as directly lower cholesterol levels are definite 'must-dos'!

Foods rich in fibre include:

- Fruits and vegetables.
- Beans and pulses.
- Cereals and grains.
- Nuts and seeds.

Types of fibre

There are two types of fibre, soluble and insoluble, and most of the benefits associated with lowering cholesterol are associated with soluble fibre, found mostly in fruits, vegetables, oats and beans. As well as lowering cholesterol levels, daily consumption of fruits and vegetables offer several additional benefits for a heart-healthy diet:

- Many of these foods are rich in antioxidants, helping to reduce cholesterol oxidation and free radical damage.

- They are lower in calories and fats, reducing abdominal obesity and Type 2 diabetes (therefore reducing the risk of heart disease and levels of oxidized LDL cholesterol).

Inulin fibre

Some fruit and vegetables contain inulin, a type of fibre which is effective at carrying cholesterol out of the body. In order to help reduce cholesterol levels, plan to include inulin-rich foods at every lunch and dinner. Inulin is fermented in the bowel, and one of the products of this fermentation is short chain fatty acids. When absorbed back into the bloodstream, these short chain fatty acids help to improve lipid metabolism and reduce circulating fats.

Inulin-rich foods:

- Chicory.
- Onion.
- Asparagus.
- Garlic.
- Jerusalem artichoke.

Consume foods rich in antioxidants

Oxidized cholesterol is a serious contributor to cardiovascular disease. However, it can be reduced by nutrients called antioxidants, and several large scale studies have illustrated that a high antioxidant intake benefits arterial health. Plant nutrients such as flavonoids have been found to have a powerful antioxidant effect.

For example, tomatoes contain a nutrient called lycopene which has been found to have several cardio-protective properties:

- It has a high antioxidant content.
- It regulates cholesterol synthesis.
- It stimulates the breakdown of 'bad' LDL cholesterol.

'Positive cholesterol-lowering results have been shown with foods such as apple, garlic, chicory and asparagus.'

≡ Low blood levels of lycopene have been linked with a higher incidence of death from heart disease.

Which foods have the highest antioxidant content?

Fresh fruits and vegetables tend to have the highest level of antioxidants, particularly berries, green vegetables and orange-coloured fruit and vegetables rich in beta carotene. Scientists in the USA measure the antioxidant power of foods and herbs using a scale called ORAC (oxygen radical absorbance capacity). The number of ORAC units indicates the amount of free radicals that a food can neutralise.

Foods with the highest ORAC antioxidant power

Food	ORAC units per 100g
Prunes	5770
Raisins	2830
Blueberries	2400
Blackberries	2036
Kale	1770
Strawberries	1540
Spinach	1260
Raspberries	1220
Brussels sprouts	980
Alfalfa sprouts	930
Broccoli	890

Antioxidants include vitamins A, C and E, minerals zinc, iron and selenium, and various phytonutrient compounds found mostly in fruits and vegetables.

Boost your vitamin A intake by eating more foods rich in beta carotene

Vitamin A is found mostly in dairy produce which often also contains saturated fats. However, beta carotene is converted into vitamin A as and when required, and is found mostly in vegetables and fruits.

Boost your beta carotene intake by:

- Including carrots, squash or pumpkin in each dinner.
- Swapping normal potato for sweet potato.
- Adding spinach, watercress or rocket to salads and sandwiches.
- Snacking on papaya, mango, cantaloupe melon, nectarines, peaches and apricots.

Boost your vitamin E intake by:

- Snacking on nuts and seeds, especially Brazil nuts, almonds and hazelnuts.
- Drizzling high-quality, cold vegetable oils on to salads.
- Adding pine nuts or sunflower seeds to salads and stir fries.
- Adding wheatgerm to cereals or yoghurts.
- Adding avocado to salad sandwiches, salads and wraps.

Boost your vitamin C intake by:

- Snacking on citrus fruits and kiwis.
- Adding berries to breakfast cereals, yoghurts and desserts.
- Munching on raw peppers in salads, sandwiches and with dips.
- Adding dark green leafy vegetables to salads, sandwiches and dinners.

Boost your zinc intake by:

- Snacking on pumpkin seeds.
- Adding wheatgerm to breakfast cereals.

'Hertog et al (1993) illustrated that risk of death from cardiovascular disease was 68% lower in those consuming the highest amount of flavonoids.'

■ Enjoying oysters or other seafood.

Best food choices for iron

Meat, offal and eggs are all iron-rich foods, but these also contain saturated fat, so if you're watching your fat intake you need to fill up on alternative iron-rich foods. Green leafy vegetables contain excellent levels of iron, but the ferric form of iron from plant sources needs the presence of vitamin C for optimum absorption, as this alters the iron molecule to a form more easily absorbed in the gut. Most iron-rich vegetables are also rich in vitamin C, but you can combine an iron-rich food with one containing vitamin C as follows.

Boost your iron intake by:

■ Adding iron-rich fenugreek or fennel seeds to green leafy vegetables.

■ Eating vitamin C-rich berries with iron-rich oats at breakfast.

■ Mixing iron-rich lentils or peas with vitamin C-rich peppers for lunch or dinner.

Boost your selenium intake by:

■ Snacking on Brazil nuts or sunflower seeds.

■ Eating plenty of brown rice.

■ Including seafood in your diet.

'Early human diets provided up to 1g per day of phytosterols, but our typical Westernised diet contains less than half of this, as we eat fewer vegetables, nuts, legumes, unrefined grains and natural vegetable oils.'

Phytosterols

Many plant foods, particularly nuts, legumes (peas, lentils, soya, peanuts, alfalfa), wholegrains and unrefined vegetable oils, are rich in natural nutrients called phytosterols, the plant equivalent of cholesterol. Splitting the word phytosterol into two helps to explain what a phytosterol is:

■ Phyto means 'plant based; to do with plants'.

■ Sterol means a type of fat, as in cholesterol.

So phytosterol is the plant version of the animal-derived cholesterol.

There are two classes of phytosterol, sterols and stanols, both known to reduce LDL cholesterol levels.

Early human diets provided up to 1 gram per day of phytosterols, but our typical Westernised diet contains less than half of this as we eat fewer vegetables, nuts, legumes, unrefined grains and natural vegetable oils.

How do phytosterols reduce cholesterol?

Phytosterols reduce cholesterol by competing for intestinal absorption with both dietary and biliary (from the liver/gall bladder) cholesterol. Anything that is not absorbed into the bloodstream or lymphatic system during digestion (therefore remaining in the gastro-intestinal tract) proceeds on to the large intestine and leaves the body in faeces. Consuming 1.5-1.8 grams per day of plant sterols or stanols can reduce cholesterol absorption by 30-40%, and 2.2 grams per day of plant sterols has been shown to reduce cholesterol absorption by 60%. With less cholesterol in the bloodstream, cells are stimulated to take up more cholesterol, resulting in increased clearance of circulating LDL. Although the decreased cholesterol absorption due to phytosterol intake also stimulates increased cholesterol synthesis in the liver, the net result is still a reduction in serum LDL cholesterol concentration.

Jenkins et al (2005) reported an average reduction in LDL cholesterol of 30% in participants following a diet including soy protein, almonds, oats, barley, psyllium husk fibre, okra and aubergine, and 1g of plant sterols daily from an enriched margarine. This reduction is not significantly different from the effects of statin drugs. However, the average LDL reduction with the same diet over one year, researched by Jenkins et al again, was only 13%, probably due to dietary adherence, although one third of the participants did still have more than a 20% reduction in LDL levels.

Ostlund et al illustrated that removing the phytosterols from corn oil increased cholesterol absorption by 38% (2002) and removing phytosterols from wheatgerm increased cholesterol absorption by 43% (2003), proving that eating phytosterol-rich foods really makes a difference to the amount of cholesterol that you absorb.

Increasing your phytosterol intake

Phytosterols and stanols are also added to some foods such as margarines to help reduce cholesterol. The next chapter discusses how you can include these functional foods in your diet and use phytosterol therapy to help lower your cholesterol levels. However, including more phytosterol-rich foods in your diet will enhance the effects of consuming foods with added sterols or stanols, so to help lower your cholesterol, make the following changes:

- Snack on nuts instead of biscuits, sweets or chocolate.

- Eat wholegrains rather than refined white flour products.

- Include more beans, pulses and legumes in your diet.

- Use unrefined vegetable oils instead of butter and refined margarine spreads.

- Swap minced beef for soya mince, or use soya products such as tofu, soya yoghurt and soya milk.

For a heart-healthy diet, eat porridge made with soya milk and added fruit for breakfast, a large salad with chicory, onion and asparagus at lunchtime, and fish with broccoli and garlic-roasted squash and carrots for dinner.

Reduced carbohydrate diets may improve cholesterol metabolism

Low carbohydrate diets have been shown to be more effective than low fat diets in reducing the amount of oxidized cholesterol in the arterial wall (Leite et al, 2010). However, although Nordmann et al (2006) reported reduced triglyceride and elevated HDL levels in reduced carbohydrate diets, total and LDL cholesterol reduced more with a low fat diet. The OmniHeart Randomized Trial (Appel et al, 2007) showed that replacing a carbohydrate-rich diet with one rich in unsaturated fat, predominantly monounsaturated fats, lowers blood pressure, improves lipid levels, and reduces estimated cardiovascular risk. A pooled analysis of 11 American and European studies (344,696 participants) found a slightly increased risk of heart disease when saturated fat was decreased and carbohydrates were increased (Jakobsen et al, 2009).

Barona et al (2011) fed a Mediterranean-style low-glycaemic-load diet to participants for 12 weeks. A significant increase in plasma lutein and β-carotene (antioxidants) was measured, with LDL cholesterol reduced from an average of 3.5 to 2.9 mmol/l (P<.0001), and VLDL and IDL also reduced. Oxidized LDL was significantly reduced by 12%, and the change in oxidized cholesterol was inversely correlated with an increase in plasma lutein, suggesting that lutein (antioxidant) concentrations may protect against oxidative stress by reducing oxidized cholesterol. Blood levels of beta carotene, another antioxidant, also increased.

Fat around the middle

There is a connection between fat stored around the middle (central obesity), disturbed blood glucose regulation and high blood pressure; having all three is a condition called metabolic syndrome or Syndrome X, and this increases your risk of heart disease and Type 2 diabetes. The excess glucose from too many cakes, pastries, sweets, chocolate and white bread products causes insulin resistance and high blood sugar. Central obesity and insulin resistance are both powerful risk factors for cardiovascular disease; with increased central obesity, hepatic (liver) production of LDL increases, leading to elevated triglyceride and apolipoprotein(b) levels and an impaired LDL: HDL ratio. All these changes exert a significant pro-thrombotic and pro-inflammatory state. In their meta-analysis and review measuring the association between metabolic disease and cardiovascular disease, Motillo et al (2010) report a two-fold increase in the risk of cardiovascular disease, stroke, and death from cardiovascular disease in those with metabolic syndrome.

'Being "apple shaped" increases your risk of poor cholesterol metabolism, heart disease and diabetes.'

Reducing carbohydrate intake

Many experts are now suggesting that carbohydrate intake should not exceed 60% of total energy intake. However, we do need carbohydrate foods for energy, fibre, essential vitamins, minerals and phytonutrients.

Follows these guidelines to get your carbohydrate intake right:

▒ Include small portions of wholegrain carbohydrates in most meals.

- Limit portion sizes of starchy carbohydrates such as rice, pasta, cereals and potatoes.

- Eat a wide range of different types of carbohydrate foods, including high-fibre, low GI beans, pulses and lentils.

- Fill up on non-starch carbohydrates such as fruits and vegetables.

- Choose lower GI carbohydrates for healthy glucose metabolism.

- Avoid or limit foods with a high GI, particularly sugary foods and refined carbohydrates such as biscuits, cakes, muffins and pastries.

Tips to help you reduce the carbohydrate load of your meals

What to reduce	What to add in
Reduce your portion size of cereal to 35g or less.	Add any low GI fruit – cherries, citrus fruits, apple, pear, cherries, prunes or strawberries.
Reduce your portion of rice to 75g or less.	Add vegetables to the rice whilst it cooks, risotto-style. Pack it out with onions, garlic, frozen peas, peppers and sweetcorn. Alternatively, cook the rice separately but add extra vegetables to the other part of your meal, packing out chilli, curry or stroganoff with vegetables containing less starch and fewer calories.
Reduce your portion of pasta to 75g or less.	Replace starchy pasta with water-rich aubergines, courgettes, tomatoes, red onions and garlic for a lower calorie and tastier Mediterranean-style meal with added health benefits!
Have fewer potatoes!	Swap potatoes for other vegetables. The bright colours of vegetables such as pumpkin, carrot, beetroot or broccoli denotes the high levels of phytonutrients in these foods, which all contain less starch and fewer calories than potatoes.

Eating a low GI diet

It isn't just the amount of carbohydrate that we eat that can present a problem, but also the type of carbohydrate foods eaten. There is an increasing body of evidence linking elevated cholesterol levels and impaired cholesterol metabolism to a diet rich in refined carbohydrates. Such a diet, based upon white bread and bakery products, and a large amount of foods with a high glycaemic index (GI), cause problems with elevated blood glucose and glucose metabolism.

Ravid et al (2008) illustrated that a high glucose concentration after a meal increases intestinal cholesterol absorption. A diet high in sugars and refined carbohydrates also contributes to conditions such as insulin resistance, metabolic syndrome and diabetes, and these conditions are all linked with increased levels of oxidative stress. Oxidative stress is linked with higher levels of oxidized cholesterol, and therefore linked with increased risk of cardiovascular disease.

How do high GI carbohydrates affect cardiovascular risk factors?

Excess carbohydrate intake or dysfunctional glucose metabolism seem to contribute to cardiovascular disease through a number of possible routes:

- High blood glucose increases LDL cholesterol.

- High blood glucose enhances oxidation of lipoprotein(a).

- Increased fat deposition as excess calories are taken in is common in diets that are high in refined carbohydrate foods which fail to 'fill you up', prompting further eating.

- Foods with a high GI also incite a higher insulin release, increasing the likelihood of excess glucose being converted into fatty acids and added to fat deposition, particularly around the middle.

- This increase in insulin release can lead to insulin resistance, which disturbs glucose metabolism further and contributes to the onset of metabolic syndrome and Type 2 diabetes, and all the aforementioned factors resulting from these conditions that heighten the risk of cardiovascular disease.

'Oxidative stress is linked with higher levels of oxidized cholesterol, and therefore linked with increased risk of cardiovascular disease.'

Does the amount or type of protein in my diet affect my cholesterol?

It is the view of many dieticians, nutritionists and trusted sources of dietary information that some aspects of the Atkins diet are unhealthy due to a high fat content and very low levels of carbohydrate and fibre. However, whilst it may not be healthy to go into ketosis with a negligible carbohydrate intake, and it is recommended that non-starch polysaccharides such as vegetables should always remain in the diet, the Atkins diet and similar reduced carbohydrate diets do illustrate some beneficial cholesterol-lowering results. However, replacing some of your carbohydrates with vegetable or fish-derived protein foods is a healthier option than eating more meat, eggs and dairy foods which all contain larger amounts of saturated fat.

The OmniHeart trial (2005) which placed 164 participants on three different diets for six weeks in a crossover trial, giving them a diet rich in carbohydrates (containing 58% energy intake from carbohydrates and 15% from protein), a protein-rich diet providing 25% of energy intake from protein foods, and a diet rich in unsaturated fat. The diet which partially replaced carbohydrates with protein reduced LDL (and HDL) cholesterol and triglycerides, and lowered blood pressure. The diet which partially replaced carbohydrates with unsaturated (mostly monounsaturated) fat had no significant effect upon LDL levels, but increased HDL cholesterol and lowered blood pressure and triglycerides. The estimated reduction in CVD risk was similar on both reduced carbohydrate diets. Approximately two-thirds of the additional protein foods on the higher protein diet in the OmniHeart trial were vegetable protein sources such as soya, legumes, nuts, seeds and grains, although some eggs, meat and dairy were also included.

What type of protein should you eat?

Mangravite et al (2011) compared two reduced carbohydrate, higher protein diets for the effects upon cholesterol and blood lipid parameters. Participants eating protein containing less saturated fat had greater reductions in total, LDL, non-HDL and apolipoprotein(b) levels than those eating protein foods containing more saturated fat. Triglycerides were reduced in both diets. Other researchers have also noted unhealthy atherosclerotic changes in arterial health following diets high in saturated fat.

Proteins and fats usually occur together in the same foods, so increasing protein consumption often increases fat intake. Animal proteins also tend to contain more saturated fats, so if you choose to increase your protein intake, take into account the following tips for the most healthy higher protein diet:

- Don't increase your intake of meats and dairy produce, as these foods contain more saturated fat. Some studies show a relationship between saturated fat intake and higher total and/or LDL cholesterol levels but many others, including a recent meta-analysis published in the American Journal of Clinical Nutrition (2010) show no apparent relationship, so in the current inconclusive climate, it recommended that you limit intake of these fats.

- Do increase vegetable proteins as these contain the types of unsaturated fats that have also shown improvements in cholesterol metabolism.

- Fish is also a healthy protein food to include in the diet due to its polyunsaturated fatty acids which have been shown to increase HDL cholesterol.

'Proteins and fats usually occur together in the same foods, so increasing protein consumption often increases fat intake.'

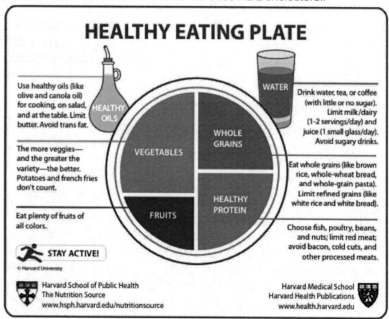

HEALTHY EATING PLATE

Use healthy oils (like olive and canola oil) for cooking, on salad, and at the table. Limit butter. Avoid trans fat.

HEALTHY OILS

WATER
Drink water, tea, or coffee (with little or no sugar). Limit milk/dairy (1-2 servings/day) and juice (1 small glass/day). Avoid sugary drinks.

The more veggies— and the greater the variety—the better. Potatoes and french fries don't count.

VEGETABLES

WHOLE GRAINS

Eat whole grains (like brown rice, whole-wheat bread, and whole-grain pasta). Limit refined grains (like white rice and white bread).

HEALTHY PROTEIN

Eat plenty of fruits of all colors.

FRUITS

Choose fish, poultry, beans, and nuts; limit red meat; avoid bacon, cold cuts, and other processed meats.

STAY ACTIVE!
© Harvard University

Harvard School of Public Health
The Nutrition Source
www.hsph.harvard.edu/nutritionsource

Harvard Medical School
Harvard Health Publications
www.health.harvard.edu

Copyright © 2011, Harvard University

For more information about The Healthy Eating Plate, please see The Nutrition Source, Department of Nutrition, Harvard School of Public Health: www.thenutritionsource.org

By following these tips and replacing refined and higher GI carbohydrates with protein foods, you are combining several dietary adjustments known to improved cholesterol metabolism. By keeping plenty of non-starch polysaccharides (vegetables, salad and fruit) and wholegrains in the diet, you are also maintaining a healthy intake of phytosterols, fibre and nutrients.

Other dietary factors that can affect your cholesterol levels

You are what you eat, and there are a number of other dietary habits that may be beneficial or detrimental to management of your cholesterol levels and affect your risk of heart disease.

Garlic

Garlic is known to have several heart-healthy properties, and onion and garlic were used in ancient Egypt, Greece and Italy for heart disease. Garlic contains a number of sulphur compounds which provide its pungent odour but are also extremely beneficial for a healthy heart:

- It contains inulin fibre which helps to reduce 'bad' LDL cholesterol.

- It reduces triglycerides (fats) in the blood.

- It 'thins' the blood, making it less likely to clot.

- It reduces blood pressure by vasodilating (widening) blood vessels.

A recent meta-analysis conducted by Zeng et al (2012) on the effects of garlic on blood lipids illustrated a significant reduction in total cholesterol and triglyceride levels. One of the main therapeutic compounds in garlic is called allicin. For this compound to be most active, the garlic should be crushed and left for up to ten minutes, then eaten raw. Crushing, slicing or pressing garlic activates the enzyme that forms the active compounds that have 'heart-healthy properties', some of which are still viable with up to six minutes of boiling or oven roasting garlic at 200ºC, so garlic still retains some therapeutic properties with light cooking if it is crushed, and the loss of anti-clotting properties can be offset by increasing the amount eaten.

To enjoy the heart-healthy benefits of garlic:

- Eat crushed, sliced or grated garlic raw.

- Crush, slice, grate or press the garlic and leave for up to ten minutes to allow the enzyme alliinase to form the active compounds.

- If cooking garlic, crush it first and allow it to rest, then cook moderately for no more than six minutes.

- Add a little raw garlic to cooked uncrushed garlic to reinstate its anti-clotting properties.

Nuts and seeds

Nuts and seeds have several properties to help reduce cholesterol.

- The vegetable protein content can help to reduce cholesterol levels, particularly when replacing refined carbohydrates in the diet.

- Nuts and seeds contain the types of unsaturated fats that appear to help create a healthy cholesterol ratio and metabolism.

- High fibre content limits cholesterol absorption in the gut, reducing overall cholesterol levels.

Flaxseeds and fenugreek seeds in particular can help to reduce cholesterol as part of a healthy diet. Kristensen et al (2012) found that adding functional foods containing flaxseeds lowered total cholesterol and LDL cholesterol by up to 12 and 15% respectively. Fenugreek seeds contain compounds called saponins that inhibit cholesterol absorption in the intestines, reduce cholesterol production by the liver, and may also raise HDL cholesterol levels. Research has shown reduced cholesterol levels after consumption of 25 to 50g of defatted fenugreek seed powder daily, although adding germinated fenugreek seeds to meals is also effective. Fenugreek powder is generally taken in amounts of 10 to 30g three times per day with meals.

'Adding raw garlic to uncrushed microwaved garlic re-instates the anti-clotting ability lost in the cooked garlic.'

Cavagnaro et. al. *Journal of Agricultural and Food Chemistry.*

Tea and coffee

Research on the effects of tea or coffee on cholesterol metabolism is limited and studies have produced conflicting results, but the majority of research seems to suggest a positive association between the polyphenols found in drinks such as tea and coffee, and a reduction in cardiovascular disease. Some research suggests that paper-filtered coffee is the best choice as far as cholesterol is concerned, but it is generally thought that too much caffeine can contribute to hypertension, so limit coffee consumption in particular to one to two cups daily, or swap to tea.

Green tea seems particularly effective, and has lower caffeine content. A meta-analysis of randomised controlled trials conducted by Zheng et al in 2011 showed that green tea reduced total and LDL cholesterol by stimulating HDL cholesterol transport back to the liver.

A word about salt

Although there appears to be no direct link between salt intake and cholesterol levels, there is certainly an association between high salt (sodium chloride) consumption and cardiovascular disease, as a high salt intake can cause hypertension, which contributes to arterial damage. Our intake and ratio of sodium to potassium is an important factor in the development of hypertension, and a low salt diet which is also high in fruit and vegetables has been proven to significantly reduce blood pressure.

> Start checking the salt content on tinned and packaged foods and choose low-salt products. A high-salt food contains more than 1.5g of salt per 100g (or 0.6g sodium per 100g), and a low-salt food contains 0.3g salt or less per 100g (or 0.1g sodium).

Ways to reduce salt intake:

- Don't add salt to cooking.
- Don't add salt to your food.

- Check food labels for high salt or sodium content and choose low-salt alternatives.

- Avoid high-salt foods such as Marmite, anchovies, salted crisps and nuts.

- Limit other foods containing salt, such as cheese, crackers, bread, pizza, sauces and tinned/packet soups and convenience foods.

- Eat plenty of potassium-rich foods to counteract the effects of sodium – fill up on fruit, vegetables and juices.

The Food Standards Agency currently recommends limiting your salt intake to 6g daily, but some food labels list sodium rather than salt content. You can calculate the amount of salt in a food by multiplying the sodium content by 2.5. For example, if a portion of food contains 0.8g sodium, it will contain about 2g of salt.

Herbs and spices

Using herbs and spices such as turmeric, cinnamon and laurel to flavour food can have several benefits:

- They may help you to reduce your salt intake.

- Some can help to reduce your cholesterol levels.

- Some also help to moderate glucose absorption, improving cholesterol metabolism through enhanced carbohydrate metabolism.

Cooking and food preparation tips to reduce cholesterol

You can also help to reduce your cholesterol by changing the way you prepare and cook food.

Use:

- Steaming.

- Poaching.

- Raw foods.

- Grilling.

- Microwaving.

Avoid:

- Frying.

- Roasting

Also, remember to reduce fat intake by:

- Cutting fat off meat.

- Using low-fat versions of dairy produce such as cheese and milk.

- Using vegetable fats such as olive oil instead of butter or ghee.

- Using phytosterol-enhanced margarines instead of butter.

- Swapping double cream for single cream, fromage frais or crème fraiche, or even better, using no fat/low-fat yoghurt or soya yoghurt.

Summing Up

- Eat more fibre: fill up on vegetables, beans, pulses, wholegrain cereals, nuts, seeds and fruits.

- Add inulin-rich foods to meals – more garlic, chicory, asparagus and artichoke.

- Eat a diet high in antioxidants to reduce oxidation of LDL cholesterol – include brightly coloured fruits and vegetables at each meal to increase your antioxidant intake.

- Fill up on phytosterol-rich foods such as nuts, legumes (peas, lentils, soya, peanuts, alfalfa), wholegrains and unrefined vegetable oils.

- Limit overall carbohydrate intake to 60% of calorie intake, eat fewer refined carbohydrates and more low GI (slow release) carbohydrates.

- If you increase your protein intake, eat more fish and vegetable protein foods (nuts, seeds, soya) rather than meat, dairy or eggs.

- Add heart-healthy garlic to your diet.

- Snack on nuts and seeds, and add them to meals.

Chapter Five

Phytosterol Therapy to Lower Cholesterol

Although we eat foods containing plant sterols (phytosterols) every day, the amount most people eat is not enough to significantly reduce the amount of cholesterol you absorb into the body. Phytosterol-enriched foods provide one of the most popular functional foods available – Benecol and Flora alone offer products such as margarines, yoghurts, yoghurt drinks, soft cheeses and juices to help reduce cholesterol levels. Plant sterols and stanols are types of phytosterol, typically found in nuts, legumes, wholegrains and unrefined vegetable oils. Consuming additional phytosterols either added to food or as supplements is called phytosterol therapy.

'Studies have shown that plant sterols in particular are most helpful in reducing existing high cholesterol levels, rather than preventing elevated cholesterol.'

Do phytosterols reduce cholesterol?

Both sterols and stanols are known to reduce LDL cholesterol levels. Consuming up to 3g of phytosterols daily in margarine, yoghurt, orange juice and other functional foods has been shown to reduce LDL cholesterol by up to 15% versus placebo, with one meta-analysis of trials showing mean reductions of 10-11%. Adding phytosterols to statin (drug) therapy has been associated with reductions of 7-20% in LDL cholesterol for up to 1.5 years (Malinowski and Gehret, 2010), although the effectiveness of phytosterols in lowering cholesterol does vary from one person to another.

The effects of phytosterol therapy are greater with advancing age and higher cholesterol levels. You may benefit from using functional foods to increase your phytosterol intake if your total cholesterol is over 5mmol/l or if you have LDL ('bad' cholesterol) of over 2.6mmol/l. The typical 2g of plant sterol added to daily portions of margarine, for example, has been shown to reduce LDL cholesterol as follows:

- An average of 0.54mmol/l reduction in people aged 50-59.

- An average of 0.43mmol/l reduction in people aged 40-49.

- An average of 0.33mmol/l reduction in people aged 30-39.

The risk of cardiovascular disease would be reduced by approximately 25% after two years in those aged 50-59.

How do phytosterols work?

Phytosterols reduce cholesterol by competing with cholesterol for intestinal absorption. More recent findings suggest that plant stanols/sterols also affect cholesterol metabolism in the intestinal cells. Another effect of reduced cholesterol uptake into the body is that with less LDL cholesterol circulating and therefore reducing the supply of cholesterol to body cells, the cellular uptake of cholesterol is enhanced, reducing the amount of circulating cholesterol even further.

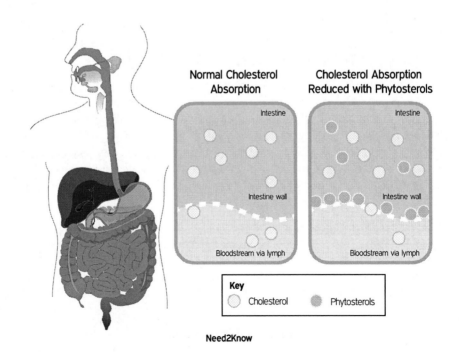

Need2Know

Plant sterols have been repeatedly proven to lower overall and low-density lipoprotein (LDL) cholesterol, although the effects are enhanced by combining sterol-enriched foods with a healthier diet.

Reduction in cholesterol from using margarines with plant sterols added	Reduction in cholesterol from using enriched margarines plus eating more vegetables, fruit, soya and nuts
Total cholesterol ↓ 10%	Total cholesterol ↓ 22.34%
LDL cholesterol ↓ 14%	LDL cholesterol ↓ 29.71%

(Buckley et al, 2007)

Other important facts about phytosterols

- Doses higher than 2 grams per day do not seem to substantially improve the cholesterol-lowering effects of plant sterols or stanols.

- Reductions are likely to be greater in those with higher baseline (starting) levels of LDL cholesterol.

- Reductions with phytosterol-enriched foods are greater in older adults.

- Phytosterols may also, as a lipid, potentially contribute to atherosclerosis, but their absorption rate is so low this does not happen.

- The cholesterol-lowering effects of plant sterols and stanols seem to last for up to one year.

Further reading of this research is available at lpi.oregonstate.edu/infocenter/phytochemicals/sterols/sterolrefs.html

How much will I need to consume to make a difference?

0.8-1.0 grams per day is the lowest dose that results in clinically significant LDL cholesterol reductions of at least 5%. A healthy diet provides approximately 160-400mg (0.16-0.4g) of phytosterols daily, and to sustain benefits from phytosterols, you need to consume at least 1g daily. If you are consuming phytosterol-enriched foods, you can follow the food manufacturer's guidelines as to how much of their products you need to consume to get up to 2g of sterol or stanol daily. This is usually equivalent to 1 yoghurt drink or 2-3 servings of spread, milk or yoghurt.

A downside to phytosterol-enriched foods

Although plant sterols have been proven to lower cholesterol, they can also reduce the absorption of some fat-soluble vitamins such as beta carotene and vitamin E. As these antioxidants help to reduce the oxidation of LDL cholesterol, this is an important consideration when consuming phytosterol-enriched foods. Phytosterols or stanols can reduce the blood concentration of beta carotene levels by 25% and vitamin E by 8%. If you don't have high cholesterol, you shouldn't be consuming phytosterol-enhanced foods, as these may reduce your cholesterol level too much as well as reducing blood antioxidant levels. Do not regularly eat foods with added phytosterols if you are:

- Pregnant.
- Breastfeeding.
- A child.

The National Heart Foundation in Australia recommends a limited consumption of added plant sterols or stanols, and advises consumption of at least one serving of carotenoid-rich foods daily to maintain carotene levels for those consuming functional foods with added plant sterols.

Carotenoid-rich foods:

- Carrots.
- Sweet potato.
- Squash and pumpkin.
- Peaches and apricots.
- Green leafy vegetables.

Foods containing vitamin E:

- Brazil nuts, almonds, pine nuts and hazelnuts.
- Vegetable oils.
- Seeds.
- Wheatgerm.
- Avocado.

Ways to consume phytosterols

- Swap butter or margarine for a spread enriched with plant sterols/stanols.
- Swap full-fat yoghurts for lower fat, phytosterol-enriched or soya yoghurts (which contain natural phytosterols).
- Choose low-fat milk also enriched with phytosterols or use soya milk.
- Eat plenty of high-fibre fruit, vegetables, oats and beans rich in natural phytosterols.
- Drink phytosterol-enriched juices.
- Include soya protein in your diet – soya milk, soya beans, soya yoghurts, tofu etc.
- Snack on nuts and seeds.

'Greater benefits will be seen if you change from butter to a plant sterol margarine, than changing from a polyunsaturated margarine.'

Make sure you make healthy changes

As elevated cholesterol levels often occur with increased body weight, eating large amounts of margarine is not the best way to consume phytosterols to reduce cholesterol, as you would be simultaneously increasing your intake of fat and calories, which may increase your weight. Some margarines contain hydrogenated or trans fats which should also be avoided, so try to get most of your phytosterols from foods that contain natural phytosterols, then top up with enriched juices or yoghurts. Phytosterol-enriched foods can be a useful, although sometimes expensive, adjunct to your diet, as they add an additional amount of plant sterols to your daily consumption. However, you should not rely upon these functional foods, but make healthy changes to your overall diet and lifestyle for maximum benefits.

Summing Up

- Phytosterols naturally occur in nuts, legumes, wholegrains and unrefined vegetable oils.

- Enriched (functional) foods that have phytosterols or stanols added to them include margarines, yoghurts, yoghurt drinks, soft cheeses and juices, which can be expensive, but can help you increase your daily intake of stanols/sterols.

- Consuming 1g-3g has been shown to reduce LDL cholesterol by up to 15% versus placebo, taking phytosterols in conjunction with statins has been associated with reductions of up to 20%, and eating a healthy diet naturally rich in phytosterols in addition to using enriched foods has been shown to reduce LDL cholesterol by almost 30%.

- Reductions in cholesterol are likely to be greater if you already have a high level of LDL cholesterol or are older.

- Phytosterols can affect absorption of fat-soluble vitamins, so increase your intake of carrots, pumpkin, squash, sweet potato, green leafy vegetables, and fruits such as mango, peach and apricot for additional beta carotene, and eat avocado, nuts and seeds for vitamin E.

Chapter Six

Supplements to Lower Cholesterol

There are a number of nutrients in foods that are known to help lower cholesterol or improve cholesterol metabolism. As our diet contains larger amounts of processed food products, many of these vital nutrients are reduced or lost, and we lose the natural benefits gained from eating a healthy diet. Making healthier food choices can help to avoid this, but sometimes taking a supplement can provide more effective and faster results.

All of the supplements discussed here have a proven effect upon cholesterol health and will have an additive effect if taken in conjunction with the dietary adaptations discussed in this book. Many of the supplements, especially phytosterols and fibre supplements, can also add to the effect of statin medication, but you should always notify your doctor or health practitioner before you begin to take any supplements in conjunction with medication, as there may be health contraindications or interactions that affect the usefulness of either the medication or the supplement.

You may benefit from taking supplements if:

* Your diet contains few vegetables, wholegrains, nuts and pulses rich in fibre and phytosterols, and you are unable or unwilling to make dietary adjustments.

* You already have a high cholesterol level.

* You are taking cholesterol-lowering medication and wish to either lower the dose or consider an alternative treatment.

* You have a family history of heart disease or have heart disease yourself.

It is essential that if you are taking any medication, or are pregnant or breastfeeding, you should consult your doctor or healthcare professional before taking any supplements. You should consult a qualified nutritionist or dietician for advice on the right supplements to reduce cholesterol.

Phytosterols and fibre

Plant fibres have the greatest amount of scientific research supporting their efficacy to reduce cholesterol.

Plant sterols and stanols

'Plant fibres have the greatest amount of scientific research supporting their efficacy to reduce cholesterol.'

In a review of double-blind trials published in the British Medical Journal (2000), Law states that sterols can reduce the risk of heart disease by up to 25%. Sterols and stanols are commonly added to margarines, yoghurts and other functional foods in order to help reduce cholesterol by competing for intestinal absorption, reducing the amount of cholesterol absorbed into the body. You can also take sterols or stanols in supplement form, and they have been shown to enhance the effect of statin drugs.

Beta sitosterol

Beta-sitosterol has been shown to reduce blood levels of cholesterol in several trials, including one by Chen at al (2009) where LDL was reduced by 12.4%, apolipoprotein(b) was reduced by 6.1% and triglycerides were reduced by 9% following the use of 3.3 grams per day of plant sterol. However, its effectiveness may be reduced if taken in conjunction with the drug ezetimibe.

Sitostanol

Sitostanol is the substance added to Benecol products, a synthetic molecule related to beta sitosterol. In one controlled trial, supplementation with 1.7 grams per day of a plant-sterol product containing mostly sitostanol, combined with dietary changes, led to a 24% drop in LDL cholesterol compared with only a 9% decrease from dietary changes (Jones et al, 1999). Many other trials show similar results. Sitostanol can also be found in some supplements.

Soluble fibre

Beta glucan

Beta glucan is the ingredient that provides oats with their cholesterol-lowering properties; its effectiveness is so evident that several regulatory bodies have approved a health claim on the cholesterol-lowering effects of oat ß-glucan at levels of 3 grams per day, allowing this information to appear on certain oat-based food products. It is a type of soluble fibre, also found in barley, and it binds with cholesterol (and bile acids), taking them out of the body with the faeces.

Results from a number of double-blind trials have illustrated reductions of approximately 10% less total cholesterol and 8% less LDL cholesterol, with HDL cholesterol often simultaneously increased, in some cases up to 16% higher. Othman et al (2011) conducted a meta-analysis of studies conducted during the past 13 years, and found that 3g or more daily of oat ß-glucan consumption was associated with reductions of 5% in total cholesterol and 7% in LDL cholesterol.

Glucomannan

Glucomannan is another type of soluble plant fibre. Sood et al (2008) conducted a meta-analysis of 14 trials to research the effects of glucomannan and found statistically significant reductions in total and LDL cholesterol, triglycerides and fasting blood glucose. Effective amounts of glucomannan for lowering blood cholesterol range between 4 to 13 grams daily.

Psyllium husk

Psyllium husk is a type of soluble fibre usually used to help alleviate constipation and normalise bowel function. However, it has been shown to have cholesterol-lowering properties, by binding with intestinal cholesterol and increasing its elimination in the faeces. Moreyra et al (2005) found that administering 15mg of psyllium husk with 10g of simvastatin was as effective as taking 20mg of simvastatin. Taking 5 to 10 grams with meals (1 to 2 teaspoons mixed with water) may help to reduce your cholesterol levels.

Soya supplementation

Soya contains phytosterols and isoflavones, naturally occurring plant components thought to have beneficial effects upon cholesterol metabolism. As well as being available in foods (soya milk, soya yoghurt, miso, tempeh and tofu), it is readily available as a supplement powder. A meta-analysis of 30 studies by Harland et al (2008) illustrated that an intake of 27g of soy protein daily resulted in significant reductions of total and LDL cholesterol. Along with several other successful trials, it is thought that approximately 30 grams a day of powdered soya protein added to food or drinks can help to lower cholesterol.

'Antioxidants stabilise free radicals, preventing oxidation to LDL cholesterol and damage to artery walls, two things thought to contribute to cardiovascular disease.'

Antioxidants

Antioxidants stabilise free radicals, preventing oxidation to LDL cholesterol and damage to artery walls, two things thought to contribute to cardiovascular disease. Antioxidants such as vitamin E are our main source of protection against oxidative damage, and it is known that certain antioxidants can reduce the risk of heart disease as well as diabetes and cancer.

Vitamin E

The cardio-protective benefits of vitamin E include its antioxidant properties, which help to prevent LDL cholesterol becoming oxidized, and it also reduces liver production of cholesterol. Although earlier studies reported vitamin E supplementation to reduce heart disease by 41%, and a 40% decrease in cholesterol oxidation after participants took 800IU of vitamin E daily for three months (Jialal and Grundy, 1992), other trials have shown no apparent effect of vitamin E. However, many doctors still recommend that everyone should supplement 400 IU of vitamin E daily to reduce the risk of having a heart attack. Vitamin E works in conjunction with vitamin C, the effects of each vitamin increased by the other, so a supplement containing both of these antioxidants may be a good idea.

Vitamin C

Vitamin C may also reduce heart disease by protecting LDL cholesterol from oxidative damage and by reducing LDL cholesterol levels. Use at least 100 mg per day to reduce LDL oxidation – some experts suggest using up to 1g (1000mg) daily.

Coenzyme Q10 (CoQ10)

This antioxidant is unlikely to affect cholesterol levels, but is included here because statin therapy reduces levels of CoQ10 in the body, which has a detrimental effect upon LDL oxidation and overall health and wellbeing. Statins work by inhibiting an enzyme that manufactures cholesterol in the liver. However, this also affects the production of coenzyme Q10. Coenzyme Q10 is found in virtually all cell membranes and, amongst many other functions, is essential for energy production in the body's cells. Together with vitamin E, CoQ10 helps to protect LDL cholesterol from oxidation, so although statins may reduce the amount of cholesterol produced, they may also increase the oxidation of LDL cholesterol, which is a greater risk factor for atherosclerosis and cardiovascular disease than the amount of circulating LDL cholesterol.

People with high cholesterol levels tend to have lower levels of CoQ10, and its natural production in the body also declines with age. There is no evidence that taking coenzyme Q10 will be beneficial to cholesterol levels, but as statins reduce levels of CoQ10, supplementing with this antioxidant will normalize levels in the body and may reduce side effects caused by statins such as muscle pain. Research has found reductions in oxidative stress in patients with coronary artery disease taking 150mg of CoQ10 daily. However, you should always consult your doctor if you experience any side effects from medication, and let them know if you are considering taking a CoQ10 supplement.

'People with high cholesterol levels tend to have lower levels of CoQ10, and its natural production in the body also declines with age.'

Other vitamins and minerals

Vitamin B3 (niacin)

1.5 to 3g of niacin daily is sometimes prescribed by doctors to help reduce cholesterol. Niacin has been shown to increase HDL levels and significantly reduce lipoprotein(a). It may also improve arterial endothelial function and reduce inflammation. Studies on niacin therapy have been almost universally favourable; however, high intakes of niacin can cause facial flushing, headaches or stomach ache, or more severe effects in some cases, and may increase the risk of muscle damage if taken in conjunction with statins. Delayed-release 'non-blushing' forms of niacin are recommended if you are taking high doses.

Niacin not only lowers LDL cholesterol and raises HDL cholesterol, but it also appears to reduce the thickness of artery walls. A study comparing the effects of niacin with the drug ezetimibe showed that those taking niacin had a significant reduction in artery thickness (therefore improving cardiovascular health), while those taking ezetimibe experienced an increase in arterial thickness.

'Vitamin B3 raises HDL "good" cholesterol by 30% to 35% and has been shown to reduce incidence of heart attacks, stroke and cardiac mortality.'

Duggal et. al. Rosalind Franklin University of Medicine and Science.

Garlic capsules

A recent meta-analysis of 26 studies by Zeng et al (2012) researching the effects of garlic on blood lipids illustrated a significant reduction in total cholesterol and triglyceride levels. The efficacy of garlic capsules relies on the supplement preparation; where the active ingredients of garlic are concentrated within a garlic capsule, cardiovascular benefits can be seen. 600 to 900mg a day of a standardised garlic extract may help lower cholesterol, reduce blood pressure and help to prevent hardening of the arteries.

Probiotics

Guo et al (2011) conducted a meta-analysis of randomised controlled trials involving 13 trials (485 participants), and found that probiotics, usually taken for digestive complaints to reinstate or rebalance the good bacteria in the gut, appeared to reduce total and LDL cholesterol. This surprising result shows that cholesterol metabolism is not entirely about the fats that we eat, but more about how our body works as a whole.

A note on supplementation

Supplements can be taken in conjunction with one another, although you should consult a qualified nutritionist for advice. Some supplements combine several different ingredients known to lower cholesterol, which can help to reduce the amount of supplements you take.

Whilst including foods rich in these nutrients will certainly benefit your health, high doses of vitamins may be necessary to benefit from some of these therapeutic effects. It is recommended that you consult a qualified nutritional practitioner for a safe and effective dietary and supplement prescription.

Summing Up

- Taking supplements to help lower cholesterol or decrease cholesterol oxidation may be helpful, particularly if you have a high cholesterol level and/or your diet is poor.

- Sterols such as beta sitosterol or sitostanol can reduce the risk of heart disease by up to 25% by reducing cholesterol absorption and altering cholesterol metabolism.

- Plant fibres such as beta glucan, glucomannan or psyllium husk can reduce the absorption of cholesterol in the gut.

- Supplementing with soya can help to reduce cholesterol levels due to its levels of isoflavones and phytosterols.

- Taking antioxidants such as vitamin E, vitamin C and coenzyme Q10 can help to reduce the oxidation of LDL cholesterol.

- Taking timed-release vitamin B3 (niacin) can increase HDL levels, significantly reduce lipoprotein(a) and reduce arterial wall thickness.

- Garlic is renowned for its heart-healthy properties and has shown significant reductions in total cholesterol and triglyceride levels.

- Always consult a qualified health practitioner for specialised help with taking supplements, and let your doctor know if you are taking medication.

Chapter Seven

Statins and Other Cholesterol Medication

In the UK, two-thirds of adults have a total cholesterol level of 5mmol/l or more (NHS), with an average total cholesterol level of 5.3mmol/l (British Heart Foundation). These figures are above the healthy guidelines given, and the UK population has one of the highest average cholesterol levels in the world. With heart disease at an all-time high, GPs are prescribing cholesterol-lowering medication to increasing numbers of patients in an attempt to reduce the risk and occurrence of heart disease, and anti-cholesterol drugs are now being sold without prescription at chemists.

But do we really need to take these drugs? Whilst cholesterol-lowering medication may help to reduce the risk of heart disease, it is not without side effects, so it is important to consider the pros and cons of medication versus lifestyle management strategies.

'The UK population has one of the highest average cholesterol levels in the world.'

Why is cholesterol medication so readily prescribed?

A high blood cholesterol level is still considered by many to be one of the most important risk factors for developing heart disease, although there are a number of other risk factors:

- Gender.
- Age.
- Family history of premature heart disease (males before age 55, females before age 65).

- Being overweight or obese.
- Smoking.
- Health (such as having high blood pressure or diabetes).
- Being of South Asian origin.

The more risk factors you have, the higher the risk of heart disease and the greater the need to reduce your cholesterol level. Although a higher cholesterol level is only one risk factor for heart disease, many people are prescribed drugs to reduce cholesterol levels even when other risk factors are not present. Cholesterol medication may also be prescribed as a preventative measure when cholesterol levels are not elevated. GPs are incentivised to put more people on statins as part of the government's campaign to reduce heart disease.

'Ideally, your total cholesterol should not be lower than 3.9 mmol/l.'

What is a healthy cholesterol level?

What constitutes a healthy cholesterol level is controversial, even amongst doctors. 'Normal' cholesterol used to be 7mmol/l, but as cholesterol-lowering drugs failed to reduce the number of deaths from cardiovascular disease, the 'normal' total cholesterol level is now considered to be 4-5mmol/l, with a target LDL cholesterol of less than 2mmol/l. However, there is no target blood cholesterol level for those who do not have, and are not at risk of cardiovascular disease.

Can cholesterol be too low?

Some authorities suggest that cholesterol should be as low as possible, even lower than the levels that naturally occur in the human body, but this requires medication to achieve, and may cause other health complaints. Ideally, your total cholesterol should not be lower than 3.9 mmol/l.

There have been several trials that have indicated links between low cholesterol and anxiety or depressed mood, and some research suggests an increase in suicide attempts. The nature of the association between mental disorders and cholesterol levels remains unclear, although there appears to be some connection. Reitz et al (2010) concluded that higher cholesterol levels

(HDL and non-HDL) are associated with a reduced risk of Alzheimer's disease. Further research is needed to determine the exact function of cholesterol in the nervous system and the effects of a reduced cholesterol level.

Effects commonly reported in conjunction with very low cholesterol levels include:

- Increased anxiety.
- Depression.
- Increased risk of cerebral stroke.
- Possible increase in mortality from cardiovascular disease.
- Increased occurrence of respiratory and digestive disease.
- Low birth weight and risk of early birth if pregnant.
- Increased risk of cancer.
- Higher death rate.

Types of cholesterol-lowering medication

Statins

Statins are the most commonly prescribed type of cholesterol-lowering medication. Statin medications include the following drugs with some brand names in brackets:

- Simvastatin (Zocor).
- Atorvastatin (Lipitor).
- Rosuvastatin (Crestor.)
- Fluvastatin (Lescol).
- Pravastatin (Lipostat).
- Simvastatin combined with ezetimibe (Inegy).

Statins are prescribed for both familial hypercholesterolaemia and elevated cholesterol levels caused by lifestyle factors. They are more effective in preventing you from having further heart attacks (secondary prevention) rather than reducing your risk of having a heart attack (primary prevention) although approximately 75% of statin prescriptions are for primary prevention. They may be prescribed if you have normal cholesterol levels, but have one or more risk factors for cardiovascular disease:

- Angina (chest pain).
- Previously had a heart attack.
- Previously had a stroke.
- Peripheral vascular disease (narrowing of blood vessels, usually in the legs).
- Diabetes and are over 40.
- Diabetes, are under 40 but have other risk factors for heart disease, such as high blood pressure or a family history of heart disease in a relative younger than 40.

'It appears that statins do not reduce the risk of cardiovascular events through lowering LDL cholesterol, but by reducing inflammation in a similar way to asprin, vitamin E or fish oils.'

How do they work?

Statins work by inhibiting a vital enzyme that manufactures cholesterol in the liver. This reduces LDL cholesterol production in the liver, which has been shown to decrease LDL cholesterol blood levels by up to 50% and enhance the removal of plasma LDL. Although this reduction in LDL cholesterol was originally thought to be the reason for reduced cardiovascular events, research now shows that statin drugs seem to affect cholesterol metabolism through antioxidant and anti-inflammatory effects.

Statins may reduce cardiovascular disease by affecting other factors involved in the development of atherosclerosis:

- Stabilising plaque formation.
- Protecting the artery endothelium.
- Enhancing anticoagulation factors which reduce blood clotting.

All these factors occur in the development of atherosclerosis following free radical or oxidative damage, which prompts an immune response causing plaque formation and blood coagulation (Rosenson, 1998). The level of C-reactive proteins (CRP) in the blood indicates the amount of endothelial damage, and statins reduce CRP levels. Lovastatin and simvastatin have been shown to inhibit LDL oxidation and uptake by macrophages (immune cells); statin therapy does not alter tissue antioxidant levels, but seems to increase blood antioxidant capacity.

Common side effects (affecting up to 1 in 10 people):

- Gastrointestinal problems such as diarrhoea, constipation, flatulence and heartburn.
- Joint pain.
- Feeling sick.
- Nerve damage.
- Insomnia.
- Headaches.
- Impaired memory.
- Inflammation, muscle pain and stiffness – if these happen your doctor may test your blood for a substance called creatinine kinase. If levels are high you may be advised to stop taking the statin and restart on a lower dose once levels of creatinine kinase have dropped.

Less common side effects include:

- Loss of appetite.
- Vomiting.
- Muscle damage.
- Peripheral neuropathy (loss of sensation or pain in nerve endings of hands and feet).
- Skin rash.

Rare side effects include:

- Dizziness.

- Hepatitis (inflammation of the liver).

- Kidney damage.

Interactions with other substances

Statins can interact with other foods, supplements and medicines such as antibiotics or warfarin, sometimes increasing the likelihood of side effects. You should ask your doctor about potential interactions with other medications or supplements such as niacin (vitamin B3).

Grapefruit juice

Grapefruit juice doesn't interact with all statins, just simvastatin and atorvastatin. Avoid drinking grapefruit juice if you are taking simvastatin as it reduces simvastatin breakdown in the liver, raising the amount in the blood and increasing the likelihood of side effects. Atorvastatin also interacts with grapefruit juice if you drink large quantities.

When to avoid statins

Statins should not be taken if you are planning a pregnancy, pregnant or breastfeeding, or have liver disease or persistently abnormal liver function blood tests. Simvastatin should not be taken if you are taking medicines that slow down the breakdown of simvastatin in the liver, such as some antibiotics and medicines for HIV.

Statins should be taken with caution if you are at greater risk of developing certain muscle disorders that cause muscle pain and breakdown of muscle tissue. These risk factors include:

- A history of liver disease.

- Drinking large quantities of alcohol.

- A history of muscle side effects when taking cholesterol medications.

'Statins should not be taken if you are planning a pregnancy, pregnant or breastfeeding, or have liver disease or persistently abnormal liver function blood tests.'

- A family history of muscle damage or some forms of kidney damage.
- Underactive thyroid if untreated or not controlled.
- Being over 70 years old.

Do statins work?

Statins are a relatively new type of drug, so the side effects and benefits from taking them are not entirely known. A review of the effects of statins involving 14 randomised controlled trials and 34,272 participants states that those with a normal cholesterol level and good health may derive no benefit from taking statins and there is no evidence to justify statin prescription in this group (Taylor et al, 2011). The British Heart Foundation has also stated that the benefits of prescribing statins for this group of people are unclear.

Non-statin cholesterol medication

Some individuals cannot tolerate statins due to the side effects, so a number of other cholesterol-lowering drugs are available. Each type of drug – and in some cases individual medications and brands in each drug class – has its own contraindications for use and side effects which your doctor will have taken into account before prescribing your cholesterol medication, so a simplified overview is given here.

Bile acid sequestrants

These include colestyramine (Questran), colesevelam (Welchol) and colestipol (Colestid).

How do they work?

They work by binding to bile acids from the liver and gall bladder (which contain biliary cholesterol), preventing it from being reabsorbed into the body, which has a knock-on effect of lowering blood cholesterol. As fewer bile acids are reabsorbed, the liver uses up more cholesterol making more bile, so reducing the amount of circulating cholesterol in this way too.

Side effects

Bile sequestrants may affect the absorption of other medications such as birth control pills, so check the best time to take your cholesterol medication or other drugs with your doctor or chemist. Side effects of this type of medication include:

- Constipation.
- Bloating.
- Stomach pain.
- Gas.
- Upset stomach.
- Vomiting.
- Diarrhoea.
- Loss of appetite.
- Heartburn.
- Indigestion.

This type of medication can also interfere with the absorption of fat-soluble vitamins A, D, E and K, so you should consider taking a supplement with long-term drug use.

Fibrates

These may be prescribed if you have a high triglyceride level, with or without a high cholesterol level. Types of fibrate drugs include:

- Bezafibrate (Bezalip, Zimbacol)
- Ciprofibrate
- Fenofibrate (Supralip)
- Gemfibrozil (Lopid)

How do they work?

Fibrates reduce the production of fats (lipids) by the liver, including cholesterol and triglycerides. Gemfibrozil increases the breakdown of triglycerides in the body, and lowers LDL cholesterol by increasing the amount expelled from the gall bladder in bile. It also increases the levels of HDL cholesterol. Ciprofibrate and fenofibrate increase levels of HDL cholesterol and decrease the production of LDL cholesterol by the liver, which causes the liver cells to take up more LDL cholesterol from the blood. They also stimulate the action of enzymes that break down triglycerides in the blood, and decrease triglyceride production in the liver.

'Fibrates reduce the production of fats (lipids) by the liver, including cholesterol and triglycerides.'

Side effects

Fibrates can increase your risk of myopathy (muscle damage), especially if taken with statins. The risk is greatest with gemfibrozil, which should not be taken with statins. Side effects include:

- Feeling sick.
- Bloating.
- Indigestion.
- Stomach pain.
- Diarrhoea.
- Loss of appetite.

※ Possible allergic reactions.

Selective cholesterol absorption inhibitors

※ Ezetimibe (Ezetrol)

How do they work?

These drugs block the absorption of dietary and biliary cholesterol in the intestine without affecting the absorption of fat-soluble vitamins, triglycerides and bile acids, which are all still absorbed. Selective cholesterol absorption inhibitors can complement the effects of statins, and may be prescribed if blood lipid levels remain high despite statin treatment, or if there are unacceptable side effects from taking statins. Cholesterol absorption inhibitors work in a different way to statins, so when co-administered with a statin they can boost the cholesterol-lowering effect. Ezetimibe can provide an additional 16-18% reduction in LDL cholesterol, a reduction equal to that achieved with an eight-fold increase in the starting dose of a statin.

Side effects

※ Headache.

※ Abdominal pain.

※ Diarrhoea.

※ Constipation.

※ Flatulence.

※ Nausea.

※ Dizziness.

※ Fatigue.

※ Allergic skin rashes.

More serious disorders such as pancreatic or gall bladder inflammation, gallstones and liver disorders are also reported as a side effect.

Other medications for cholesterol

Other medicines used include anion exchange resins, such as Questran, which increase the excretion of LDL cholesterol by preventing its reabsorption from the intestine. A combined treatment with statins, anion exchange resins and diet can reduce the total cholesterol level in the blood by 30-40% and the LDL cholesterol by a greater amount.

Interactions with other substances

Phytosterols

You can take phytosterol-enriched foods in conjunction with cholesterol medication, although you should let your GP know, as the effects should be cumulative and your cholesterol medication prescription may need adjusting.

Should you be taking cholesterol-lowering drugs?

Some experts believe that the lower cholesterol is, the lower the risk of heart disease, and if side effects of cholesterol-lowering drugs appear minimal, it's better to take them. However, other experts argue that there is no benefit for those in lower risk groups, and have concerns about some of the side effects, such as damage to muscles or the kidneys. This opinion seems to be supported by the recent Cochrane review by Taylor et al.

Summing Up

- The UK population has one of the highest average cholesterol concentrations in the world, and in an attempt to reduce heart disease GPs are incentivized to prescribe cholesterol-lowering medication to increasing numbers of patients.

- Although some still consider a high total and LDL cholesterol level to be a risk factor for cardiovascular disease, there are several other risk factors that should be taken into account when calculating one's risk of heart disease. The more risk factors you have, the greater the need to reduce your cholesterol level.

- Your doctor is likely to prescribe cholesterol-lowering medication if your total cholesterol is greater than 4-5mmol/l or LDL cholesterol is more than 2mmol/l or if you have other risk factors for cardiovascular disease.

- Total cholesterol should not be lower than 3.9 mmol/l.

- Statins are the most common type of cholesterol-lowering medication prescribed, although they appear to work by reducing inflammation and oxidation, not because of their cholesterol-lowering effects.

- Other types of cholesterol-lowering medication may be prescribed alone or in conjunction with statins.

- All types of cholesterol-lowering medication have side effects.

- You should aim to make dietary and lifestyle changes to support the effects of cholesterol-lowering medication – doing so may even mean a reduction in your drug prescription. These changes may include phytosterol therapy.

Chapter Eight

Lifestyle Habits That Affect Your Cholesterol Levels

A number of lifestyle habits affect cholesterol production and the way that we manage and use cholesterol in the body. The amount of exercise we do, how much alcohol we consume, whether we smoke and how well we deal with stress all affect our cholesterol metabolism, so there are a number of positive lifestyle changes you could make which will have a positive effect upon your health and risk of cardiovascular disease.

How exercise affects cholesterol levels

In addition to reducing your risk of heart disease by reducing heart rate and blood pressure, regular exercise can help decrease levels of LDL cholesterol and triglycerides, and increase levels of HDL cholesterol. Having higher levels of HDL (good) cholesterol in the bloodstream enhances the 'clearing' of excess cholesterol out of the blood and reduces the risk of cardiovascular disease. Exercise also reduces the occurrence of other conditions which seem to promote poor cholesterol metabolism, such as obesity and Type 2 diabetes.

Recent research comparing the effects of medium and high intensity exercise illustrated significant reductions in LDL, total cholesterol and cholesterol/HDL ratio, and in those doing high-intensity exercise, HDL cholesterol was also increased (Sheikholeslami et al, 2011).

'Just being overweight increases the likelihood of having elevated blood cholesterol and triglycerides.'

Benefits of regular exercise

If you exercise regularly you are more likely to have:

- Lower levels of total cholesterol.
- Lower levels of LDL cholesterol.
- Higher levels of HDL cholesterol.
- Lower levels of triglycerides.

In addition to lower blood pressure and better blood glucose metabolism, you are also likely to have a lower body weight, lower body mass index and a healthier waist to hip ratio.

'As well as using up fat for energy, regular exercise also reduces, or helps you to cope better with stress – both of these effects have a beneficial effect upon cholesterol metabolism.'

Does regular exercise reduce LDL and/or risk of cardiovascular disease?

The simple answer is that it does both. In repeated trials, regular exercise has been shown to reduce LDL cholesterol and increase HDL cholesterol. Whether a deterioration and increased number of cardiovascular events in those with existing heart disease is reduced because of less LDL cholesterol in the bloodstream, or because of other effects of exercise, remains to be proven. As exercise reduces oxidized LDL, this is certainly favourable. Overall effects improving cardiovascular health are likely to be from a number of positive metabolic and inflammatory changes in the body as listed below.

- Lower blood pressure – resulting in less damage to artery walls.
- Better glucose regulation – resulting in less inflammation and C-reactive protein.
- Reduced deposition of adipose tissue (especially fat around the abdomen) – resulting in less inflammatory markers and reduced oxidative stress.
- Fewer inflammatory markers in the bloodstream such as C-reactive protein, indicating less inflammation from free radical damage, and/or more antioxidants, with the result of less oxidized LDL cholesterol.
- Reduced amount of circulating triglycerides as fats are used up for energy, reducing the overall risk of cardiovascular disease.

How much exercise do I need to do?

You should aim to do 30 minutes of exercise 5 times a week. You can split up the 30 minutes into smaller bouts of activity, doing three ten minute brisk walks throughout the day, for example. The intensity of the exercise should be enough that you feel warm and a little out of breath. On a scale of 1 to 10 of exercise intensity, you should aim to exercise at around a 7, although if you haven't exercised for a while you should start off at a lower intensity and gradually build up the duration and difficulty level.

Vasankari et al (1998) showed the following results in participants doing 3 and a half to 4 hours of exercise weekly for 10 months:

▓ HDL cholesterol increased by 15% in men and 5% in women.

▓ LDL cholesterol decreased by 10% in men and 11% in women.

▓ Concentrations of oxidized LDL fell by 23%.

▓ Total cholesterol and triglyceride concentrations remained unchanged.

Vuorimaa et al (2005) illustrated that long duration but low-intensity walking has beneficial effects upon blood lipid profiles. He showed the following results from two days walking for six hours each day:

▓ Oxidized LDL decreased by 25%.

▓ LDL cholesterol decreased by 14%.

▓ Total cholesterol decreased by 3%.

▓ Triglycerides decreased by 22%.

▓ HDL cholesterol increased by 9%.

Ways to do more exercise

It can be difficult to maintain a regular exercise regime, but there are a number of psychological tools that can help you to create a regular exercise habit.

Up to 80% of people do not have the 'self management' skills to continue with regular exercise without some sort of support system, explaining why many of us stop and start exercise many times over the years.

Enjoy exercise!

It is essential that you find something that you enjoy doing – if you don't enjoy it, you won't keep it up. There is an activity or type of exercise out there for everyone . . . you just need to find out what you enjoy doing. Take a look at the types of exercise below and plan how you could fit something you enjoy into your lifestyle.

Types of exercise:

* Walking/hiking.
* Swimming.
* Cycling.
* Jogging/running.
* Gardening.
* Dancing.
* Fitness classes such as Zumba, yoga, aerobics, step, body conditioning.
* Martial arts classes.
* Circuit training.
* Golf (walking round the course, not riding a golf buggy!).
* Tennis, badminton or squash.
* Football, rugby, basketball, netball.

Exercising with others

One of the most successful ways to stick with regular exercise is to exercise with other people. This is for a number of reasons:

* It takes your mind off the exercise.
* It can relieve boredom.
* It makes the exercise more enjoyable and sociable.

- You are less likely to miss an exercise session if you are letting someone else down.

- There may be an element of friendly competition.

- A bit of moral support helps!

Dissociation

For some people, exercise dissociation (taking your mind off of what you are doing) is the only way that they will stick to a regular exercise regime. Take a look at these common ways of 'switching off' and see if any of them suit you:

- Listening to music whilst you exercise.

- Watching TV in a gym.

- Chatting with a friend whilst you exercise.

- Concentrating your mind on something else whilst you exercise – revision, work problems, hitting exercise targets you've set for yourself.

Fitting more activity into your life

Just being more active will help you to manage your weight and help to reduce cholesterol levels. Here are some ways to increase daily activity:

- Use the stairs rather than the lift.

- Don't send emails to office colleagues, walk to see them to give them a message.

- Don't drive – walk if you can.

- Park further away in car parks and walk to where you're going.

- Get off the bus, tube or train a stop early.

- Walk the children to school.

- Take up an active hobby such as dancing or gardening.

- Take the dog (or other people's dogs) for a walk.

- Even housework helps to increase your overall amount of activity.

'Some research has shown that 90% of us prefer to exercise with others, and we are up to 22% less likely to stop exercising if we exercise with other people.'

Reducing body weight reduces your cardiovascular risk

Simply losing weight through exercise (or diet) will reduce your risk of heart disease. A group of researchers in the Atherosclerosis Research Team at Oakland Hospital in California tested the effects of weight loss on atherogenic lipoprotein profiles in overweight men. Weight loss reduced the level of small, dense LDL particles linked with increased atherosclerosis risk, and the greater the weight loss, the greater the cholesterol normalization, illustrating that weight loss alone can reduce the risk of cardiovascular disease.

Alcohol and cholesterol

'Wear a pedometer to measure how many steps you take each day – then set yourself daily or weekly goals to increase the amount you do.'

A few studies have found that people who drink alcohol in moderation have lower rates of heart disease. Even with elevated cholesterol levels, people in many Mediterranean countries have a lower incidence of cardiovascular events. Data from at least twenty countries in Europe, North America, Asia and Australia shows a 20 to 40% lower incidence of coronary heart disease amongst those that consume a moderate amount of alcohol, in comparison with non-drinkers or heavy drinkers. There appears to be a U-shaped relationship between alcohol consumption and heart disease, with a decreased risk of heart disease in those consuming one to two drinks daily.

It seems that despite having arterial damage caused by fatty plaques and high blood pressure, this damage is somehow offset by having a greater degree of 'relaxation' in the artery walls and less blood clotting. This appears to be due to consumption of one to two glasses of red wine daily, and is partly due to polyphenols such as resveratrol in the grapes used to make the wine. These plant nutrients appear to have a protective effect upon the artery walls which reduces the risk of a stroke or heart attack, possibly due to their antioxidant properties. So red wine won't necessarily lower your cholesterol levels, but may reduce the risk of cardiovascular events.

Moderate drinking – no more than two drinks a day – has also been shown to raise HDL cholesterol levels, and been linked to a reduced risk of blood clots and decreased levels of inflammatory markers.

Several studies show that the active component responsible for reduced cardiovascular disease is the polyphenols present in red wine, and the majority of research shows more positive results with wines from areas of south western France and the Mediterranean.

Why is red wine a heart-healthy drink?

- The ethanol (alcohol) exerts a relaxing effect upon the artery walls which allows the artery to expand and accommodate elevated blood flow and higher blood pressure, preventing damage to the artery wall that might create further atherosclerosis, and helping to prevent a cardiovascular event.

- Drinking one to two alcoholic beverages daily can increase HDL cholesterol by approximately 12%, improving your overall cholesterol ratio as the HDL cholesterol counteracts the level of LDL cholesterol.

- The flavonoid antioxidants in red wine limit the oxidation of LDL cholesterol, which is the type of cholesterol linked with arterial cholesterol deposits, so protecting the artery walls from atherosclerosis.

- The red wine polyphenols also have an anti-inflammatory effect and limit clot formation.

Although a small amount of alcohol may reduce heart disease, consuming more than one to two drinks daily is detrimental to good health, but if you do drink:

- Limit consumption to one to two drinks daily.

- Have a few days alcohol-free each week.

- Choose red wine.

Risks of drinking alcohol

Consuming too much alcohol can increase blood pressure, increase your risk of heart disease and stroke, contribute to obesity, and increase levels of triglycerides in the blood. Alcohol contains 7 calories per gram, so is almost as calorific as fat, and as a liquid, it can be easy to consume a large volume of it. This affects cholesterol metabolism in several ways:

- It contributes to central obesity, which not only increases cholesterol oxidation, but also increases the risk of developing Type 2 diabetes, metabolic syndrome and heart disease.

- It affects blood glucose metabolism, increasing the risk of insulin resistance and Type 2 diabetes, both linked with increases in oxidized LDL cholesterol.

- Alcohol is metabolised into saturated fats and if not used for energy or stored as adipose tissue, these fats may be used to help build the cell walls in artery linings. The flexibility of cell walls with greater proportions of saturated, hydrogenated or trans fats is reduced, as opposed to enhanced flexibility found with greater proportion of polyunsaturated fats. This reduced flexibility contributes to arteriosclerosis (hardening of the arteries) and leads to arterial damage.

Non-alcoholic alternatives to red wine

So if you don't already drink, don't start! You can enjoy the antioxidant benefits of polyphenols by drinking red/purple coloured fruit juices or eating the fruit itself:

- Red grape juice.
- Acai berry juice.
- Cherry juice.
- Cranberry juice.
- Prune juice.

Smoking and cholesterol

Smoking has two direct effects upon cholesterol metabolism:

- It lowers HDL cholesterol levels.
- It causes free radical damage in the body, using up antioxidants that could have reduced the oxidation of LDL cholesterol.

However, cigarette smoking contributes to heart disease in several other ways, and is responsible for approximately 20% of all deaths from heart disease.

'Patients with cardiovascular disease received red grape extract or placebo – relaxation of the brachial artery was enhanced 70% for the red grape extract group.'

Lekakis et. al.
Department
of Cardiology,
University General
Hospital, Greece.

- It increases the calcification and rigidity of artery walls, leading to arteriosclerosis.

- Nicotine speeds up the heart rate and causes the arteries to narrow, increasing blood pressure.

- The increased blood pressure can cause damage to artery walls, contributing to atherosclerosis.

- Smoking can also cause thrombotic plaques to rupture, leading to a blood clot, stroke or heart attack.

Did you know?

Your risk of cardiovascular disease (CVD) greatly increases with the number of cigarettes you smoke

You are at greater risk of CVD the longer you smoke

If you smoke a pack of cigarettes a day, you have more than twice the risk of heart attack than non-smokers.

Help to stop smoking

There are many self-help books or websites and support groups to help you to stop smoking. See *Stopping Smoking – The Essential Guide* (Need2Know) and the help list for more information.

Stress and cholesterol

There appears to be a connection between elevated stress levels and cholesterol levels. Steptoe and Brydon (2005) illustrated significant increases in total cholesterol, low-density lipoprotein (LDL) and high-density lipoprotein (HDL) cholesterol following moderately stressful behavioural tasks, which accurately predicted higher cholesterol levels in those with higher stress responses three years later. Those in the top third of stress responders were three times more likely to have higher LDL cholesterol than those in the bottom third of stress responders.

'You can halve your risk of having a heart attack within one year by stopping smoking.'
British Heart Foundation.

How does stress elevate cholesterol levels?

- Release of the stress hormones adrenaline and cortisol trigger cholesterol production in the liver to provide the body with fuel and to help repair damaged cells. However, further research is required in order to fully understand the relationship between stress, cholesterol levels and increased risk in cardiovascular disease. There are a number of theories and factors to consider when understanding the connection between stress and cholesterol:

- Increased fats (including cholesterol) and glucose in the blood may increase the risk of atherosclerosis if they aren't used up for energy. This will depend on what type of stress you are under – if you are stressed at work or home, and not very active, these additional fuels will not be used up as they would be if you were putting your body under the physical strain of 'flight or fight'.

- Release of glucose and fats into the bloodstream requires the liver to produce and secrete more LDL, increasing the amount of LDL that may become oxidized.

- Another theory is that stress interferes with clearing fats from the bloodstream because increased secretion of the stress hormones reduces fat and glucose storage.

- Research indicates that unused glucose released during chronic stress and converted into triglycerides (fats) is more likely to be stored in or around the abdomen, causing central obesity. Central obesity increases LDL production in the liver and is linked with increased levels of inflammatory markers in the bloodstream, creating a pro-thrombotic and pro-inflammatory state in the body.

- Stress is known to increase inflammatory processes and inflammatory markers in the bloodstream such as C-reactive protein, and this has been linked to elevated cholesterol levels and increased risk of cardiovascular disease.

Reducing stress and dealing with stress

How we deal with stress seems to be more important than the amount of stress we have, and some experts say that there are different 'stress personalities'. Those more capable of coping with stress have been shown to have higher levels of HDL cholesterol.

If you can identify the thing(s) causing you stress (stressors) and deal with those, this can reduce the amount of stress in your life. However, whether you can deal with your stressors or not, there are many ways to reduce stress, or help you to cope with it:

- Regular exercise.
- Yoga.
- Listening to music.
- Listening to relaxation CDs.
- Reading or listening to audio books.
- Gardening.

You might also benefit from seeing a counsellor or therapist to help you deal with stress.

A final note on creating your personal healthy cholesterol plan

There are genetic differences in how individuals react to various lifestyle factors, and this needs to be taken into account when creating your personal cholesterol plan. Considerations include:

- How your blood cholesterol levels react to the amount of cholesterol you eat.

- How your blood lipids and cholesterol levels react to the amount and types of fats that you eat.

- Your body weight and amount of central (abdominal) fat accumulation.

- How much exercise you can do.

- Whether you smoke.

- How much stress you are subjected to and how well you deal with it.

- Genetic and family health history.

'Consuming up to 2.5g of plant sterols daily can lower cholesterol absorption by 10%, but this is enhanced by another 5% if you eat a healthy diet and make lifestyle changes such as exercising regularly.'

It is worth noting that not everyone that eats a high-fat diet develops high cholesterol levels, and not everyone with elevated cholesterol develops cardiovascular disease.

Therefore, recommendations for dietary adaptations and cholesterol-lowering medication should be individualized.

However, it is worth considering that the dietary adaptations alone outlined in this book can significantly decrease the risk of cardiovascular disease, and also reduce total/LDL cholesterol levels, which may be beneficial even if this limits the amount of LDL cholesterol available to become oxidized. In addition, consuming natural or enriched foods containing plant sterols, and doing regular exercise to reduce body weight if required can normalize cholesterol metabolism in most individuals, without the side effects of cholesterol-lowering medication.

Summing Up

▨ Regular exercise reduces heart rate, blood pressure, LDL cholesterol and triglycerides, and increases levels of HDL cholesterol.

▨ Regular exercise also promotes better blood glucose metabolism, lower body weight, lower body mass index and a healthier waist to hip ratio.

▨ Maintaining a healthy weight helps to normalize cholesterol levels.

▨ One to two drinks of alcohol a day has also been shown to raise HDL cholesterol levels and been linked to a reduced risk of blood clots and decreased levels of inflammatory markers, but drinking more than this contributes to increased obesity, fatty liver and unhealthy cholesterol metabolism.

▨ Smoking lowers HDL cholesterol levels and uses up antioxidants that could have reduced the oxidation of LDL cholesterol.

▨ Individuals who are less capable of dealing with stress are three times more likely to have higher LDL cholesterol levels and lower HDL cholesterol.

Appendix A

A therapeutic diet to reduce cholesterol

Monday

Breakfast Porridge made with soya milk with almonds, linseeds and fruit.
Mid-morning Home-made hummus (chickpeas, olive oil, garlic) with celery, raw asparagus, chicory and peppers.
Lunch Lentil and tomato soup with oat cakes.
Dinner Baked salmon steak with broccoli, cauliflower and baked sweet potato.

Tuesday

Breakfast Soy yoghurt with flaked almonds, linseeds and cherries.
Mid-morning Celery, tomato and pepper crudités.
Lunch Mixed bean and brown rice salad with tomatoes, garlic, onions, fenugreek seeds, sunflower seeds, cucumber, chicory and radish.
Dinner Seared tuna steak with garlic-roast parsnips and carrots, and broccoli.

Wednesday

Breakfast Granola (toasted oats and seeds) with mixed seeds and nuts, and added fruit.
Mid-morning Soy yoghurt sprinkled with linseeds and mixed berries.
Lunch Sardines with chicory, onion, garlic, asparagus, tomatoes, celery and beetroot.
Dinner Savoy cabbage stir fry and red onion, garlic, peppers, fenugreek and other seeds, peppers and baby corn. Soya tofu or lean turkey strips may be added. Serve stir fry on its own or with brown rice.

Thursday

Breakfast — Oatabix or other oat-based cereal with soya milk, soya yoghurt and sprinkled with almonds and linseeds.

Mid-morning — Nut/seed bar.

Lunch — Peppered mackerel with a large mixed salad with chicory and fenugreek seeds.

Dinner — Stuffed peppers with a large green salad or baked beans.

Friday

Breakfast — Large fruit salad with soy yoghurt and mixed seeds.

Mid-morning — Oat cakes with hummus, celery, raw peppers and asparagus.

Lunch — Omega-3 enriched organic eggs (2) poached, served with asparagus.

Dinner — Mixed bean chilli with brown rice.

Saturday

Breakfast — Omega-3 enriched organic egg with wholegrain toast and phytosterol-enriched spread.

Snacks — Handful of nuts.

Lunch — Lentil and vegetable soup with oatcakes.

Dinner — Sweet potato and chick pea curry with brown rice or quinoa.

Sunday

Breakfast — Kedgeree made with mackerel and brown rice, chopped onion and garlic.

Mid-morning — Phytosterol-enriched or soya yoghurt sprinkled with mixed seeds.

Lunch — Baked sweet potato with hummus and a large salad.

Dinner — Salmon, sweet potato and asparagus risotto.

Note – Fenugreek powder could be added to porridge, soups, stews or yoghurts for additional cholesterol-lowering benefits. Phytosterol-enhanced functional foods such as margarines or yoghurts may also be eaten in place of standard margarines or yoghurts. Vegetable oils may be drizzled onto salads. Drink green tea or a soya-based drink.

Appendix B

Recipes

Kedgeree

Serves 2

Ingredients
100g brown rice
2 haddock/mackerel fillets
2 omega-3 enriched organic eggs, boiled or poached

Method
1. Cook the rice as usual.
2. Meanwhile poach the fish in water or skimmed milk.
3. Mix the cooked brown rice with the flaked fish.
4. Place chopped boiled egg or poached egg on top and add some fresh coriander or dill.

Lentil and tomato soup/lentil and vegetable soup

Serves 2

Ingredients
100g of lentils, tinned or pre-cooked
1 tablespoon olive oil
1 onion, grated
1 red chilli, deseeded and chopped
2 garlic cloves, crushed
Half a pint of vegetable stock
2 tablespoons chopped parsley, coriander or basil
8 medium tomatoes, chopped

Method
1. Heat the oil and soften the onion.
2. Add the chilli and garlic and heat for another minute.
3. Add the chopped tomatoes and cook for 10 minutes.
4. Add the stock and lentils, bring to the boil and then simmer for 20 minutes (alternatively, this can be cooked in a slow cooker on low for 5-6 hours).
5. Puree the soup in a blender and serve, adding the freshly chopped parsley or basil.

Any other vegetable can be used in addition to, or instead of the tomatoes.

Salmon and sweet potato risotto

Serves 2

Ingredients
2 salmon steaks
2 cloves garlic, finely diced
1 handful of asparagus, lightly boiled, grilled or roasted
2 medium-sized sweet potatoes, roasted
1 onion, sliced
150g organic brown rice or risotto
Olive oil

Method
1. Bake the salmon steak and roast the sweet potato in olive oil.
2. Meanwhile, cook the risotto as follows: sauté some garlic and onion in a pan with a little olive oil.
3. Add the rice, stirring to coat it with the oil/onion/garlic mixture, then add water and allow it to simmer, gradually adding water as required until the rice is cooked. If you have parboiled the sweet potato before roasting, use this water.
4. Once the rice is cooked add the sweet potato, asparagus and baked salmon to the risotto and serve.

Savoy cabbage stir fry

Serves 2

Ingredients
1 onion
2 garlic cloves
1 savoy cabbage
A handful of mushrooms
A handful of frozen peas
A handful of sweetcorn
A handful of peppers
1 portion of tofu, chicken or turkey (optional)
1 tablespoon of fenugreek or mixed seeds

Method
1. Heat a little olive oil in a pan.
2. Add the chopped onion and the cloves of sliced garlic.
3. Any herbs or spices can also be added at this time (such as chopped chilli, turmeric, oregano or ginger).
4. Cut the savoy cabbage into thin strips and add this to the pan.
5. Once the onion and cabbage are slightly browned, add the other vegetables, seeds and optional tofu or grilled lean meat and cook through.

Mixed bean chilli

Serves 2-4

Ingredients
A selection of beans/lentils, soaked – choose from any type of beans and lentils, and combine a selection to make up 200g-250g dry weight
1 onion, chopped
2 cloves of garlic, chopped
1-2 chillies, chopped
A handful of mushrooms
2 carrots, diced
A handful of frozen peas and sweetcorn
A handful of fresh/frozen peppers
1 tin of tomatoes
A cupful of fresh tomatoes
75g organic brown rice per person

Method
1. Soak a selection of beans overnight.
2. While boiling the beans, brown the onion and garlic in a little olive oil then add the fresh chillies.
3. Add the mushrooms, carrots and other vegetables to the dish with the tinned tomatoes.
4. Simmer for one hour, adding the beans halfway through.
5. Tinned tomatoes should be added, along with fresh tomatoes if desired, and any other vegetables, lentils and other pulses not requiring pre-soaking.
6. Serve with brown rice.

Sweet potato and chickpea curry

Serves 2

Ingredients
1 tsp olive oil
2 cloves garlic
1 onion
Handful of fresh coriander
2 tsp turmeric
2 red chillies, chopped
2 carrots
1 large sweet potato
3 large fresh tomatoes
1 vegetable stock cube made into 300ml
1 small tin of chickpeas
1 head of broccoli
1 small pot fat-free Greek yoghurt

Method
1. Heat the oil, cooking the garlic and onion until soft.
2. Add the turmeric and chillies.
3. Stir and cook for two minutes.
4. Add carrots, sweet potato and tomatoes.
5. Add the liquid stock and chickpeas, bring to the boil and then simmer for approximately 20 minutes.
6. Meanwhile, blanch the broccoli and add once the curry is cooked. Remove from the heat; allow to cool slightly before adding the yoghurt.
7. Sprinkle a generous helping of fresh coriander on top and serve with brown rice (60g per person, uncooked weight).

Stuffed peppers

Serves 2

Ingredients
2 potatoes
1 tsp of olive oil
2 cloves of garlic, chopped
1 handful each of mushrooms, fresh or frozen sweetcorn and peas
1 onion, chopped
100g fresh spinach
2 large peppers, raw, with tops cut off
1 dessert spoon of mixed seeds – fenugreek, linseed, pumpkin, sunflower and sesame seeds
Green salad

Method
1. Bake the potatoes until cooked.
2. Meanwhile, heat a little oil and lightly stir fry the garlic, mushroom and onion.
3. Add the seeds, peas and sweetcorn and heat through, adding the spinach.
4. Stir until the spinach is wilted and remove from the heat.
5. Cut off the top of the potatoes and scoop out the mash into the stir fry and mix.
6. Once thoroughly mixed, stuff the peppers and potatoes with the stir fry mixture and bake for 35 minutes at to 180°C/356°F/Gas Mark 4.
7. Serve with a large green salad.

Seared tuna steak with stir fry vegetables

(Try swapping tuna steak for swordfish or marlin steaks in this recipe.)

Serves 2

Ingredients
1 handful of mushrooms
2 cloves of garlic
1 onion
1 tsp olive oil
1 fresh pepper
1 cupful of mixed sweetcorn and peas
1 tsp sesame seeds
2 tuna steaks

Method
1. Chop the mushrooms, garlic and onions and add to a tsp of heated olive oil in a pan.
2. Once browned, add the chopped peppers, sweetcorn and peas, and cook through.
3. Add the seeds and heat for a further few minutes until just browned.
4. Meanwhile, sear the tuna steak in a non-stick pan. You could rub chopped chilli and garlic onto the fish beforehand if you wish.
5. Serve the vegetables and tuna together.

Glossary

Antioxidant
Compounds or nutrients with antioxidant properties counteract free radical oxidation in the body. Examples include beta carotene, vitamins C and E, zinc and selenium.

Apolipoproteins
Apolipoproteins are proteins that bind fats together to form lipoproteins, molecules which carry cholesterol and other fats around the body. Apolipoproteins act as 'keys' for cholesterol receptors on cell membranes, enabling the delivery of cholesterol to the body cells.

Arteriosclerosis
Hardening of the artery walls caused by oxidative damage, smoking and intake of too many trans, hydrogenated and saturated fats in place of unsaturated fats.

Atherogenic
Something that can increase the risk of, or cause atherosclerosis.

Atherosclerosis
Atherosclerosis is the build-up of a waxy plaque formed from inflammatory proteins, oxidized cholesterol and other fats on the inside of blood vessels.

Artery endothelium
The smooth inner wall of an artery.

Cardiovascular disease
A term relating to diseases of the heart and blood vessels, including coronary heart disease, atherosclerosis, arteriosclerosis and thrombosis.

Carotenoids
A group of nutrients with therapeutic and antioxidant properties found predominantly in orange-coloured fruits and vegetables such as apricots, mango, carrots and sweet potato. Also found in beetroot and dark green leafy vegetables.

Cholesterol
A type of fat found in foods and made in the body.

Cholesterol ratio

A measure of cholesterol 'health', calculated by dividing total cholesterol by HDL cholesterol. A low ratio is considered more healthy.

Chylomicrons

The largest and lowest density molecule which transports fats from the digestive tract to the liver.

C-reactive protein (CRP)

A protein found in the blood – levels rise in response to inflammation within the body.

Creatinine kinase

An enzyme which speeds up the attachment of phosphate to creatine in order to create creatine phosphate, a substance used to fuel energy pathways.

Deep vein thrombosis

Thrombosis (blood clots) in the veins, usually in the legs.

Dyslipidaemia

An abnormal amount of lipids (cholesterol and other fats) in the bloodstream.

Fatty acid

Fats in food are formed from triglycerides, which are formed from a molecule of glycerol and three fatty acids. Each fatty acid is either saturated, monounsaturated or polyunsaturated, depending upon the number of hydrogen atoms and degree of saturation. Fatty acids such as omega-3 or omega-6 fatty acids have various therapeutic roles in the body.

Flavonoids

A group of compounds with anti-allergic, antibacterial, antioxidant and anti-inflammatory properties. Anthocyanidins, isoflavonoids and catechins are all types of flavonoid, commonly found in onions, apples, red wine and tea.

Free radicals

Unstable molecules or atoms which can cause damage in the body, for example, damage the artery walls.

Glucose

The main monosaccharide (sugar) found in food, which is used in the human body as a major source of fuel.

Glycaemic index

The glycaemic index (GI) is a measure of how quickly the glucose in foods is absorbed into the bloodstream – a low GI will mean the food has low glucose content or contains mostly slow-release starches. A high GI score indicates a food provides energy more quickly.

HDL cholesterol

The 'good' type of cholesterol formed from high-density lipoproteins (HDL). High-density lipoproteins carry cholesterol back to the liver, reducing blood cholesterol levels and aiding cholesterol removal via the liver and gall bladder out of the body.

Hydrogenated fat

A type of processed fat that originated as a liquid polyunsaturated fat, but has become saturated after being passed through hydrogen so that hydrogen atoms attach to the fatty acid and create a synthetic saturated fat.

Hypercholesterolaemia

This term refers to a high cholesterol level, usually used with genetic (familial) high cholesterol levels.

Hyperglycaemia

A high level of glucose in the blood.

Hyperlipidaemia

A high level of lipids in the bloodstream.

Hypertension

Consistently high blood pressure above the normal 120/80 blood pressure.

Hypoglycaemia

Hypoglycaemia is low blood sugar, when there is not enough glucose in the bloodstream for normal functioning.

Impaired glucose metabolism

Too little or too much glucose in the bloodstream as a result of many combined factors including diet and insulin resistance.

Intermediate-density lipoprotein (IDL)

A type of lipoprotein molecule that carries cholesterol. Some intermediate-density lipoproteins return to the liver but others are converted into low-density lipoproteins.

Inulin

A type of plant fibre that is useful for reducing cholesterol absorption in the digestive tract, found in chicory, Jerusalem artichokes, garlic and asparagus.

Linoleic acid

One of the fatty acids essential for good health.

Linolenic acid

The other fatty acid essential for good health.

Lipid

Another term meaning fats.

LDL cholesterol

Low-density lipoprotein (LDL) is known as 'bad' cholesterol as it is this type of cholesterol that becomes oxidised and can contribute to atherosclerosis, the 'furring' of the arteries.

LDL receptors

Receptors on cells that allow LDL cholesterol access into the cell.

Meta-analysis

A type of research where the results of a number of independent research trials are statistically combined to provide an 'average' or 'overview' of the results of a particular hypothesis.

Metabolic syndrome

A combination of central obesity, disturbed blood glucose regulation and high blood pressure, also called Syndrome X. Metabolic syndrome increases your risk of heart disease and Type 2 diabetes.

Monosaccharide

Monosaccharides are the building blocks of carbohydrate foods. When carbohydrates are digested, they are eventually broken down into these single sugars, of which the most common is glucose.

Monounsaturated fat

A type of fatty acid with one double bond in its structure, typically found in high amounts in olives, olive oil and avocados. Because there is only one double bond in these fatty acids they limit oxidation (when oxygen atoms connect to a fatty acid) when heated, reducing the risk of oxidation of fats, and free radical oxidation in the body.

Oxidation

There are several different chemical reactions which cause oxidation, but within the subject area of nutrition, oxidation is referring to unstable atoms or molecules attaching to neighbouring molecules or cells and destabilising them. This can result in a chain reaction of molecular damage causing cell damage. Heated and processed fats (trans and hydrogenated fats) are most likely to become oxidized.

Oxidized cholesterol

Cholesterol, usually LDL cholesterol, that has been oxidized (denatured).

Phytosterol

Plant derivative of cholesterol which competes for absorption with the animal sterol cholesterol, reducing cholesterol absorption into the body. Phytosterols are commonly found in plant oils, and often added to margarines and yoghurts in order to reduce cholesterol levels.

Plaque

A build-up of oxidized cholesterol and fats, and white blood cells, found on the inside of arteries causing the condition known as atherosclerosis.

Polyphenol

A group of nutrients found in abundance in dark red or purple fruits and vegetables such as red grapes, cherries and berries containing compounds with therapeutic antioxidant properties.

Polysaccharide

A number of monosaccharide sugars joined together to form a chain. Some polysaccharides form digestible starch in the diet, others form non-digestible compounds known as fibre.

Polyunsaturated fat

A type of fatty acid with more than one double bond in the structure typically found in high amounts in fish, nuts, seeds and oils such safflower or sunflower oil. The number of double bonds in these unsaturated fatty acids make them liable to oxidation when heated which is why monounsaturated oils are deemed more healthy to cook with.

Primary dyslipidaemia
Primary dyslipidaemia refers to genetic abnormalities such as familial hypercholesterolaemia.

Probiotics
The 'good' bacteria normally found in the digestive tract.

Refined carbohydrate
A type of carbohydrate that has been highly processed; usually foods such as pastries, cakes and biscuits containing white flour.

Refined fat
A type of fat that has been highly processed, such as hydrogenated, partially hydrogenated and trans fats.

Saturated fat
A type of fatty acid with no double bond in the structure typically found in meats and dairy produce, and also some vegetable foods such as coconut. The complete molecular saturation makes these fats less liable to oxidation but saturated fats are more likely to contribute to heart disease.

Secondary dyslipidaemia
Secondary dyslipidaemia refers to disturbed lipid balance caused by other factors such as lifestyle or medication.

Stanols and sterols
Plant stanols and sterols are natural plant nutrients which may be added to foods such as margarines, yoghurts and soft cheeses to help reduce cholesterol.

Thrombosis
A thrombus is a blood clot. Thrombosis is the formation or presence of a thrombus in the blood vessels.

Total cholesterol
This is the sum of the HDL, LDL, IDL and VLDL cholesterol circulating in your bloodstream.

Trans fat
A type of chemically altered fat formed during hydrogenation. The term 'trans' refers to the arrangement of atoms around the double bond(s); the structure of a trans fat aids saturation and prevents enzymes or other substances attaching to the fatty acid, denaturing its natural functions.

Triglyceride
Triglycerides are the 'building block' of fats.

Very low-density lipoprotein (VLDL)
This type of cholesterol makes up approximately 10-15% of total cholesterol and part of it is converted into LDL cholesterol.

Help List

Organisations

British Association for Applied Nutrition and Nutritional Therapy (BANT)

27 Old Gloucester Street, London WC1N 3XX
Telephone: 08706 061284
theadministrator@bant.org.uk
www.bant.org.uk
BANT is a professional body for nutritional therapists and those working in the field of nutritional science. A list of registered practitioners can be found on the BANT website.

British Heart Foundation

Greater London House, 180 Hampstead Road, London NW1 7AW
Tel: 020 7554 0000
Fax: 020 7554 0100
Heart Help Line: 0300 330 3311 (open Monday to Friday 9am-6pm)
internet@bhf.org.uk
www.bhf.org.uk
You can download information booklets on how to cope with elevated cholesterol, phytosterols and cholesterol medication from the British Heart Foundation website.
For a booklet on lowering your blood cholesterol:
www.bhf.org.uk/publications/publications-search-results.aspx?m=simple&q=cholesterol
For a booklet on how high cholesterol can increase your risk of cardiovascular disease:
www.bhf.org.uk/heart-health/conditions/high-cholesterol.aspx

NHS

Visit this NHS website for information on cholesterol and more helpful links.
www.nhs.uk/livewell/healthyhearts/pages/cholesterol.aspx
Visit this site for advice and information, or for a free Quit Kit to stop smoking.
www.smokefree.nhs.uk

QUIT

Quit is a UK charity to help people stop smoking.
www.quit.org.uk

Websites providing information on cholesterol

BBC – Health: Cholesterol

A website providing basic information about cholesterol.
www.bbc.co.uk/health/physical_health/conditions/cholesterol1.shtml

BUPA

A website providing basic information about cholesterol.
www.bupa.co.uk/individuals/health-information/directory/c/cholesterol

The Cholesterol Truth

A website providing information on alternatives to cholesterol-lowering medication.
www.thecholesteroltruth.com/

Harvard School of Public Health – The Nutrition Source

This web link provides in depth information and research about cholesterol, the effects of diet on cholesterol, and cholesterol metabolism.
www.hsph.harvard.edu/nutritionsource/what-should-you-eat/fats-full-story/index.html#references

Linus Pauling Institute

A website providing information and research on cholesterol metabolism and phytosterols.
lpi.oregonstate.edu/infocenter/phytochemicals/sterols/#intro

Patrick Holford website

Type in cholesterol to find information and advice on lowering your cholesterol level naturally through diet and supplementation. There is an option to join up as a member to have access to more information.
www.patrickholford.com/

ProLipid.com

A website with extensive information on cholesterol and heart disease, with cholesterol converters, research, diet and lifestyle tips and information on cholesterol medication.
www.prolipid.com/

General health information including information on elevated cholesterol levels and cholesterol-lowering medication

www.bupa.co.uk

www.heartuk.org.uk/

www.medicinenet.com

www.netdoctor.co.uk

www.nhs.co.uk

www.patient.co.uk/health/Cholesterol.htm

Supplement providers

Archturus

Archturus, Strathenry House, Leslie, Fife KY6 3HY
Tel: 01592 620 865
www.archturus.co.uk
Email: orders@archturus.co.uk

Biocare

Biocare Ltd., Lakeside, 180 Lifford Lane, Kings Norton, Birmingham B30 3NU
Tel: 0121 433 3727
www.biocare.co.uk
Email: biocare@biocare.co.uk

Nutrigold

Nutrigold Ltd., PO Box No. 217, Exmouth, EX8 9AX
Tel: 0845 603 5675 (local rate)
www.nutrigold.co.uk
E-mail: talk2us@nutrigold.co.uk

Book List

Encyclopedia of Natural Medicine
By Michael Murray and Joseph Pizzorno, Three Rivers Press, 1998.

Food for Health – The Essential Guide
By Sara Kirkham, Hodder, 2010
A well-researched and referenced guide to eating for health, including a chapter on eating for a healthy heart and cardiovascular system and a chapter on improving blood glucose regulation, both conditions linked with elevated cholesterol levels.

Foods that Harm, Foods that Heal
By Readers Digest, Readers Digest Assoc., 2004.
A useful guide to foods to eat and foods to avoid for a wide range of conditions.

GI How to succeed using a Glycaemic Index diet
By Harper Collins, HarperCollins Publishers, Glasgow, 2005.
A comprehensive guide to the glycaemic index of foods.

Teach Yourself Lose Weight, Gain Energy, Get Healthy
By Sara Kirkham, Hodder, 2010
A topical guide to eating a superfood diet that promotes overall good health and a healthy weight. It also includes a chapter on detoxification for liver support.

The Mediterranean Diet
By Marissa Cloutier and Eve Adamson, HarperCollins, 2004.

The Optimum Nutrition Bible
By Patrick Holford. Piatkus,1997.

Weight Loss – The Essential Guide
By Sara Kirkham, Need2Know, 2010
The ultimate guide to helping you lose weight and improve your cholesterol metabolism from doing so.

What Colour is Your Diet?
By David Heber, HarperCollins, 2001.
A great little book packed with information on the phytonutrients in food.

References

Barona J, Jones JJ, Kopec RE, Comperatore M, Andersen C, Schwartz SJ, Lerman RH, Fernandez ML.
'A Mediterranean-style low-glycemic-load diet increases plasma carotenoids and decreases LDL oxidation in women with metabolic syndrome'.
Journal of Nutritional Biochemistry, 2011.
Available at: www.ncbi.nlm.nih.gov/pubmed/21775117.

Chen SC, Judd JT, Kramer M, Meijer GW, Clevidence BA, Baer DJ.
'Phytosterol intake and dietary fat reduction are independent and additive in their ability to reduce plasma LDL cholesterol'. Lipids, 2009, Volume 44, Issue 3: 273-81.
Available at: www.springerlink.com/content/a61445x4h1w7326w/.

Duggal JK, Singh M, Attri N, Singh PP, Ahmed N, Pahwa S, Molnar J, Singh S, Khosla S, Arora R.
'Effect of niacin therapy on cardiovascular outcomes in patients with coronary artery disease'. Journal of Cardiovascular Pharmacology and Therapeutics, 2010, Volume 15, Issue 2: 158-66.

Guo Z, Liu XM, Zhang QX, Shen Z, Tian FW, Zhang H, Sun ZH, Zhang HP, Chen W.
'Influence of consumption of probiotics on the plasma lipid profile: a meta-analysis of randomised controlled trials'. Nutrition, Metabolism and Cardiovascular Diseases, 2011, Volume 21, Issue 11: 844-50.
Available at: www.ncbi.nlm.nih.gov/pubmed.

Harland JI, Haffner TA.
'Systematic review, meta-analysis and regression of randomised controlled trials reporting an association between an intake of circa 25 g soya protein per day and blood cholesterol'. Atherosclerosis, 2008, Volume 200, Issue 1: 13-27.
Available at: www.atherosclerosis-journal.com/article/S0021-9150(08)00247-5/abstract.

Hertog MG, Feskens EJ, Hollman PC, Katan MB, Kromhout D.
'Dietary antioxidant flavonoids and risk of coronary heart disease: the Zutphen Elderly Study'. Lancet, 1993, Volume 342, Issue 8878: 1007-11.

Available at: www.ncbi.nlm.nih.gov/pubmed/8105262.

Hooper L, Summerbell CD, Thompson R, Sills D, Roberts FG, Moore H, Davey Smith G.
'Reduced or modified dietary fat for preventing cardiovascular disease'. Cochrane Database of Systematic Reviews, 2011, Volume 7: CD002137.
Available at: onlinelibrary.wiley.com/doi/10.1002/14651858.CD002137.pub2/pdf/standard.

Hulthe J and Fagerberg B.
'Circulating oxidized LDL is associated with subclinical atherosclerosis development and inflammatory cytokines (AIR Study)'. Arteriosclerosis, Thrombosis and Vascular Biology, 2002, Volume 22, Issue 7:1162-7.
Available at: atvb.ahajournals.org/content/22/7/1162.long.

Jakobsen MU, O'Reilly EJ, Heitmann BL, Pereira MA, Bälter K, Fraser GE, Goldbourt U, Hallmans G, Knekt P, Liu S, Pietinen P, Spiegelman D, Stevens J, Virtamo J, Willett WC, Ascherio A.
'Major types of dietary fat and risk of coronary heart disease: a pooled analysis of 11 cohort studies'. The American Journal of Clinical Nutrition, 2009, Volume 89, Issue 5: 1425-32.
Available at: www.ajcn.org/content/89/5/1425.full.pdf+html.

Jenkins DJ, Kendall CW, Marchie A, Faulkner DA, Wong JM, de Souza R, Emam A, Parker TL, Vidgen E, Trautwein EA, Lapsley KG, Josse RG, Leiter LA, Singer W, Connelly PW.
'Direct comparison of a dietary portfolio of cholesterol-lowering foods with a statin in hypercholesterolemic participants'. The American Journal of Clinical Nutrition, 2005, Volume 81, Issue 2: 380-387.
Available at: www.ajcn.org/content/81/2/380.long.

Jones PJ, Ntanios FY, Raeini-Sarjaz M, Vanstone CA.
'Cholesterol-lowering efficacy of a sitostanol-containing phytosterol mixture with a prudent diet in hyperlipidemic men'. The American Journal of Clinical Nutrition, 1999, Volume 69, Issue 6: 1144-50.
Available at: www.ajcn.org/content/69/6/1144.full.pdf+html.

Kristensen M, Jensen MG, Aarestrup J, Petersen KE, Sondergaard L, Mikkelsen MS, Astrup A.

'Flaxseed dietary fibers lower cholesterol and increase faecal fat excretion, but magnitude of effect depend on food type'. Nutrition and Metabolism, 2012, Volume 9, Issue 1: 8.
Available at: www.ncbi.nlm.nih.gov/pubmed/22305169.

Lekakis J, Rallidis LS, Andreadou I, Vamvakou G, Kazantzoglou G, Magiatis P, Skaltsounis AL and Kremastinos DT.
'Polyphenolic compounds from red grapes acutely improve endothelial function in patients with coronary heart disease'. European Journal of Cardiovascular Prevention and Rehabilitation, 2005, Volume 12, Issue 6: 596-600.
Available at: www.ncbi.nlm.nih.gov/pubmed/16319551.

Malinowski JM, Gehret MM.
'Phytosterols for dyslipidemia'. American Journal of Health-System Pharmacy 2010, Volume 67, Issue 14:1165-73.
Available at: www.ncbi.nlm.nih.gov/pubmed/20592321.

Mensink RP and Katan MB.
'Effect of dietary fatty acids on serum lipids and lipoproteins. A meta-analysis of 27 trials'. Arteriosclerosis and Thrombosis, 1992, Volume 12, Issue 8: 911-9.
Available at: atvb.ahajournals.org/content/12/8/911.full.pdf.

Mangravite LM, Chiu S, Wojnoonski K, Rawlings RS, Bergeron N, Krauss RM.
'Changes in atherogenic dyslipidemia induced by carbohydrate restriction in men are dependent on dietary protein source'. The Journal of Nutrition, 2011, Volume 141, Issue 12: 2180-5.
Available at: www.ncbi.nlm.nih.gov/pubmed/22031660.

Mensink RP, Zock PL, Kester AD, Katan MB.
'Effects of dietary fatty acids and carbohydrates on the ratio of serum total to HDL cholesterol and on serum lipids and apolipoproteins: a meta-analysis of 60 controlled trials'. The American Journal of Clinical Nutrition, 2003, Volume 77, Issue 5: 1146-55.
Available at: www.ajcn.org/content/77/5/1146.full.pdf+html.

Mottillo S, FilionKB, Genest J, Joseph L, Pilote L, Poirier P, Rinfret S, Schiffrin EL, Eisenberg MJ.
The Metabolic Syndrome and Cardiovascular Risk. The Journal of the American College of Cardiology, 2010, Volume 56, Issue 14: 1113 – 1132.
Available at: www.sciencedirect.com/science/article/pii/S0735109710026380.

Moreyra AE, Wilson AC, Koraym A.
'Effect of combining psyllium fiber with simvastatin in lowering cholesterol'.
Archives of Internal Medicine, 2005, Volume 165, Issue 10 :1161-6.
Available at: www.ncbi.nlm.nih.gov/pubmed/15911730.

*Palomäki A, Pohjantähti-Maaroos H, Wallenius M, Kankkunen P, Aro H,
Husgafvel S, Pihlava JM, Oksanen K.*
'Effects of dietary cold-pressed turnip rapeseed oil and butter on serum lipids,
oxidized LDL and arterial elasticity in men with metabolic syndrome'. Lipids in
Health and Disease, 2010, Volume 9, Issue 137.

*Ravid Z, Bendayan M, Delvin E, Sane AT, Elchebly M, Lafond J, Lambert M,
Mailhot MG, Levy E*
'Modulation of intestinal cholesterol absorption by high glucose levels: impact
on cholesterol transporters, regulatory enzymes, and transcription factors'.
American Journal of Physiology – Gastrointestinal and Liver Physiology, 2008,
Volume 295, Issue 5: G873-G885.
Available at: ajpgi.physiology.org/content/295/5/G873.full.pdf+html.

Reitz C, Tang MX, Schupf N, Manly JJ, Mayeux R, Luchsinger JA.
'Association of higher levels of high-density lipoprotein cholesterol in elderly
individuals and lower risk of late-onset Alzheimer disease'. Archives of
Neuroogy, 2010, Volume 67, Issue 12: 1491-7.
Available at:
www.ncbi.nlm.nih.gov/pmc/articles/PMC3065942/pdf/nihms279865.pdf.

Rosenson RS, Tangney CC.
'Antiatherothrombotic properties of statins: implications for cardiovascular
event reduction'. JAMA, 1998, Volume 279, Issue 20: 1643-50.
Available at: jama.ama-assn.org/content/279/20/1643.full.pdf+html.

*Sanclemente T, Marques-Lopes I, Fajó-Pascual M, Cofán M, Jarauta E, Ros E,
Puzo J, García-Otín AL.*
'Naturally-occurring phytosterols in the usual diet influence cholesterol
metabolism in healthy subjects'. Nutrition, Metabolism and Cardiovascular
Diseases NMCD, 2011.
Available at: www.ncbi.nlm.nih.gov/pubmed/21703833.

Sheikholeslami Vatani D, Ahmadi S, Ahmadi Dehrashid K, Gharibi F.

'Changes in cardiovascular risk factors and inflammatory markers of young, healthy, men after six weeks of moderate or high intensity resistance training'. The Journal of Sports Medicine and Physical Fitness, 2011, Volume 51, Issue 4: 695-700.
Available at: www.ncbi.nlm.nih.gov/pubmed/22212275.

Siri-Tarino PW, Sun Q, Hu FB, Krauss RM.
'Meta-analysis of prospective cohort studies evaluating the association of saturated fat with cardiovascular disease'. The American Journal of Clinical Nutrition, 2010, Volume 91, Issue 3: 535-46.
Available at: www.ajcn.org/content/91/3/535.long.

Siri-Tarino PW, Williams PT, Fernstrom HS, Rawlings RS, Krauss RM.
'Reversal of small, dense LDL subclass phenotype by normalization of adiposity'. Obesity, 2009, Volume 17, Issue 9: 1768-75.
Available at: www.ncbi.nlm.nih.gov/pmc/articles/PMC2837149/pdf/nihms176454.pdf.

Sood N, Baker WL, Coleman CI.
'Effect of glucomannan on plasma lipid and glucose concentrations, body weight, and blood pressure: systematic review and meta-analysis'. The American Journal of Clinical Nutrition, 2008, Volume 88, Issue 4: 1167-75.
Available at: www.ajcn.org/content/88/4/1167.full.pdf+html.

Stanhope KL, Bremer AA, Medici V, Nakajima K, Ito Y, Nakano T, Chen G, Fong TH, Lee V, Menorca RI, Keim NL, Havel PJ.
'Consumption of fructose and high fructose corn syrup increase postprandial triglycerides, LDL-cholesterol, and apolipoprotein-B in young men and women'. The Journal of Clinical Endocrinology and Metabolism, 2011, Volume 96, Issue 10: 1596-605.
Available at: www.ncbi.nlm.nih.gov/pubmed/21849529.

Staprans I, Pan X, Rapp J, Feingold K.
'The role of dietary oxidized cholesterol and oxidized fatty acids in the development of atherosclerosis. Molecular Nutrition & Food Research, 2005, Volume 49, Issue 11: 1075–1082.

Steptoe A and Brydon L.
'Associations between acute lipid stress responses and fasting lipid levels 3 years later'. Health Psychology, 2005, Volume 24, Issue 6: 601-7.

Available at: www.ncbi.nlm.nih.gov/pubmed/16287406.

Taylor F, Ward K, Moore THM, Burke M, Davey Smith G, Casas JP, Ebrahim S.
'Statins for the primary prevention of cardiovascular disease (Review).'
Cochrane Database of Systematic Reviews, 2011, Issue 8.
Available at: onlinelibrary.wiley.com/doi/10.1002/14651858.CD004816.pub4/pdf/standard.

United States Department of Agriculture. USDA Food Surveys.
Available at: www.ars.usda.gov/Services/docs.htm?docid=14392.

US Department of Health and Human Services. National Institutes of Health/National Heart, Lung and Blood Institute.
'Your Guide to Lowering your Cholesterol with TLC – Therapeutic Lifestyle Changes'.
Available at: www.nhlbi.nih.gov/health/public/heart/chol/chol_tlc.pdf.

Vasankari TJ, Kujala UM, Vasankari TM, Ahotupa M.
'Reduced oxidized LDL levels after a 10-month exercise program'. Medicine and Science in Sports and Exercise, 1998, Volume 30, Issue 10: 1496-501.
Available at: www.ncbi.nlm.nih.gov/pubmed/9789849.

Verhagen SN, Wassink AMJ, Van der Graaf Y, Gorter PM, Visseren FLJ.
'Insulin resistance increases the occurrence of new cardiovascular events in patients with manifest arterial disease without known diabetes'. Cardiovascular Diabetology, 2011, Volume 10, Issue 100.
Available at: www.cardiab.com/content/pdf/1475-2840-10-100.pdf.

Vuorimaa T, Ahotupa M, Irjala K, Vasankari T.
'Acute prolonged exercise reduces moderately oxidized LDL in healthy men'.
International Journal of Sports Medicine, 2005, Volume 26, Issue 6: 420-5.
Available at: www.ncbi.nlm.nih.gov/pubmed/16037882.

Willett WC, Stampfer MJ, Manson JE, Colditz GA, Speizer FE, Rosner BA, Sampson LA, Hennekens CH.
'Intake of trans fatty acids and risk of coronary heart disease among women'.
Lancet, 1993, Volume 341, Issue 8845: 581-5.
Available at: www.ncbi.nlm.nih.gov/pubmed/8094827.

Zeng T, Guo FF, Zhang CL, Song FY, Zhao XL, Xie KQ.